Third Editio..

THE EXPERT WITNESS

by
Jean Graham Hall
[LL.M. (London) FCIArb MAE]
A retired Circuit Judge,
previously a Metropolitan Stipendiary Magistrate
and formerly a probation officer and social worker.
Member of the Honourable Society of Gray's Inn

and

Gordon D. Smith
[FRICS, ACIArb MAE]
Chartered Surveyor; Fellow of the Rating Surveyors
Association
Member of the London Rent Assessment Panel

First published by
Barry Rose Law Publishers Ltd

THE EXPERT WITNESS

Third Edition

XPL Edition ISBN 1 85811 374 1

Former ISBN
Barry Rose Edition ISBN 1 902 681 26 6

Published by:

XPL Law
99 Hatfield Road
St Albans,
AL1 4JL, UK

Contents

Foreword to the First Edition

By
The Rt. the Hon. Lord Justice Mustill
of Pateley Bridge
One of Her Majesty's Lords of Appeal in Ordinary.

Nowadays there seems to be almost as many law books as there are lawyers. In the main they are almost indistinguishable, except as to title: long, worthy, rather dull, and lacking in focus. Perusal gives no clear picture of those who are intended to profit from reading them, and is certainly not a pleasure.

The present work is refreshingly different. It is not long. Although it is worthy, it is without the deadening overtones so often associated with this word. It is certainly not dull, being written in an accessible and open style. The readership at which it is aimed is easy to discern: as is the function which the book is intended to fulfil: not to furnish grist for the intense analysis of recondite issues, but to give professionals without extensive experience of the adversarial way of resolving disputes a practical introduction to the problems which they are likely to face, and to the ways in which they should prepare for and perform their various functions. As such it fills a real need.

This book is a welcome departure, and I wish it every success.

Mustill
House of Lords

Preface to the First Edition

The principal aim of this book is to provide guidance and encouragement for the expert who is a newcomer to personal participation in legal proceedings in his or her professional role. (From here on, we have reduced the phrase "his and her" to the masculine only, to avoid this clumsy phrase.)

We have tried to provide a straightforward guide to help him through what is seen by many as a maze of procedures, professional etiquette and legislation. It is our hope that the result of studying the book carefully will create a confidence in one's ability to successfully convey professional knowledge and opinions to the tribunal, particularly in a first case.

We make no apology for quoting from P.D. James, doyenne of British crime writers who displayed a sure understanding of the role of the expert witness in her novel: *Death of An Expert Witness* (published by Faber & Faber Ltd, 1977). In the following extract a police inspector is referring to the work of forensic scientists:

"The defence doesn't always accept the scientific findings. That's the difficult part of the job, not the analysis but standing alone in the witness-box to defend it under cross-examination. If a man's no good in the box, then all the careful work he does here goes for nothing."

At the same time the authors trust that experienced expert witnesses will also gain some benefit from the more esoteric sections of the book.

In working together from different backgrounds professional disciplines and viewpoints, the co-authors admit to finding pleasure in discovering that the same underlying principles apply to all expert witnesses in the many - and increasingly diverse - fields of professional skills.

Jean Graham Hall
Gordon D. Smith

Note to the Third Edition

The authors respectfully dedicate the Third Edition of this book to the Rt. Hon. Lord Woolf whose clear thinking and drive have been instrumental in bringing about some badly needed changes to the subject of expert evidence.

The changes have been the inspiration behind the Third Edition and it is our hope that not only have we accurately reflected these but also that the book will prove helpful to practitioners in the new ambience of dispute resolution.

Cases Cited

List of Statutes

STATUTORY INSTRUMENTS

CHAPTER 1

Emergence of the Expert Witness

"Believe one who has proven it. Believe the expert."
Virgil: *The Aeneid*

The history of the expert in court is a long and honourable one. However, expert witnesses began to play their modern role in the eighteenth century. The foundation of the relevant rule was laid down by Lord Mansfield in *Folkes v. Chard* [1782] 3 Doug. KB 157, ie, the opinion of scientific men upon proven facts may be given by men of science within their own science. When such a person is called as a witness, his opinion is admissible on any relevant matter. If the subject does not require specialist knowledge, expert evidence will generally be excluded.

In *Folkes v. Chard* the matter before the court was whether the demolition of a sea bank, erected in 1758 for the purpose of preventing the sea overflowing into some meadows, contributed to the decay of the harbour; and the question for the court was: "To what has this decay been owing? Was it due to the bank, because it prevented the backwater?" As Lord Mansfield explained: "This is a matter of opinion; the whole case is a question of opinion, from facts agreed upon." The defendants called Mr Smeaton, an eminent engineer, to show that, in his opinion, the bank was not the cause of the mischief and that cutting the bank would not remove it. Lord Mansfield said:

"It is objected that Mr Smeaton is going to speak, not to facts, but as to opinion. That opinion, however, is deduced from facts which are not disputed; the situation of banks, the course of tides and of winds, and the shifting of sands. His opinion, deduced from all these facts is that, mathematically speaking, the bank may contribute to the mischief, but not sensibly. Mr Smeaton understands the construction of harbours, the causes of their destruction and how remedied ... I have myself received the opinion of Mr Smeaton respecting mills, as a matter of science. The cause of the decay of the harbour is also a matter of science, and still more so, whether the removal of the bank can be beneficial. Of this, such men as Mr Smeaton alone can judge. Therefore, we are of the opinion that his judgment, formed on facts, was proper evidence."

Is the Witness *Peritus* (ie, expert)?

One of the questions in *R. v. Silverlock* [1894] 2 QB 766, where it was necessary to prove handwriting by comparison, was whether the person giving evidence need be a professional expert, or a person whose skill in the comparison of handwriting had been gained in the way of his profession or business. The solicitor who gave evidence on the comparison said that since 1884, quite apart from his professional work, he had given considerable study and attention to handwriting and especially to old parish registers and wills and had, on several occasions, professionally compared handwriting, but had never given evidence on the subject. Lord Russell CJ said: "It is true that the witness who is called upon to give evidence must be *peritus*; he must be skilled in doing so; but we cannot say he must have become *peritus* in the way of his business or in any definite way. The question is, is he *peritus?* Is he skilled? Has he an adequate knowledge? Looking at the matter practically, if a witness is not skilled the Judge will tell the jury to disregard his evidence."

R. v. Silverlock was followed in the Canadian case of *R. v. Bunnis* [1964] 50 WWR 422 where the question was whether a police officer, who had made a special study of the matter, could give admissible evidence on the physiological effects of alcohol on the body. It was argued for the defence that such evidence would only be admissible from a duly qualified medical practitioner. However, Tyrwitt Drake CCJ held that so long as a witness satisfies the court that he is skilled, the way in which he acquired his skill is immaterial:

> "The test of expertness, so far as the law of evidence is concerned, is skill, and skill alone, in the field of which is sought to have the witness's opinion... I adopt, as a working definition of the term 'skilled person', one who has by dint of training and practice, acquired a good knowledge of the science or art concerning which his opinion is sought ... It is not necessary, for a person to give opinion evidence of a question of human physiology, that he be a doctor of medicine."

The question of whether a police officer was an expert in a particular field also arose in *R. v. Oakley* [1980] 70 Cr App R 7. Police officers who spend their time in the traffic division of the force are normally not regarded as experts on the theory of why accidents occur. However, in this case, a police constable with 15 years' experience in the traffic division, who had passed a qualifying examination as an accident investigator after attending a course and who had attended more than 400 fatal road accidents, was allowed to give opinion evidence of his observations at the scene of the collision. He produced a plan which he had prepared and gave expert evidence about his theories and conclusions. The appellant was convicted and appealed on the ground that the constable's evidence, which related to his opinion, had been wrongly admitted. Lord Lane CJ said:

> "We would like to make it quite clear straight away that there is no question of a police constable being prevented from giving evidence as an expert if the subject in which he is giving evidence as a expert is a subject in which he has expert knowledge, and if it is restricted and directed to the issues in the case... The answer is that as long as he keeps within his reasonable expertise, which is a matter for the Judge, he is entitled to be heard on every aspect as an expert, to that extent, if no further."

Thus we repeat that it is for the Judge to determine whether the witness has undergone such a course of special study, or possesses such experience, as will render him expert in that particular subject.

Expert Opinion must be Founded on Facts

In *R. v. Turner* [1975] QB 834 the defendant was convicted of murder and sentenced to life imprisonment. The ground of his appeal was that the Judge had refused to admit evidence which a psychiatrist was prepared to give in support of his defence of provocation, and on his behalf the Court of Appeal was asked to receive that evidence. Lawton LJ said: "Before a court can assess the value of an opinion it must know the facts upon which it is based. If the expert has been misinformed about the facts or he has taken irrelevant facts into consideration or has omitted to consider relevant ones, the opinion is likely to be valueless." He went on to say that in the judgment of the Court of Appeal, counsel calling an expert should, in examination-in-chief, ask his witness to state the facts upon which his opinion is based, and it is wrong to leave the other side to elicit the facts in cross-examination. Lawton LJ reiterated that the foundation of these rules was laid by Lord Mansfield in *Folkes v. Chard*, and was well laid, i.e. the opinion of scientific men upon proven facts may be given by men of science within their own science.

Expert Opinion may still be Admissible even where the Facts are not Agreed

An interesting old case is *Beckwith v. Sydebotham* [1807] 2 Camp 116. The *SS Earl of Wycombe*, on her homebound journey from Pictou, Nova Scotia met with stormy weather and was obliged to put into Halifax, being so disabled as to be unfit to continue the voyage. On the question as to whether evidence should be accepted from the shipwrights as to the state of the ship, Lord Ellenborough held: "Where there was a matter of skill, a science to be decided, the jury might be assisted by the opinion of those peculiarly acquainted with it from their professions or pursuits. As the truth of the facts stated to them was not certainly known, their opinion might not go for much; but was still admissible." The report continues: "The witnesses were then examined, but did not give any decided opinion."

An Expert Opinion need not be Accepted

In *Davie v. Magistrates of Edinburgh* [1953] SC 34 the Court of Session repudiated the suggestion that the Judge or jury is bound to adopt the views of the expert, even if they should be uncontradicted because "the parties have invoked the decision of a judicial tribunal and not an oracular pronouncement by an expert." The point was made clear by Lord President Cooper:

> "Expert witnesses, however skilled or eminent, can give no more than evidence. They cannot usurp the function of the jury or Judge sitting as a jury, any more than a technical assessor can substitute his advice for the judgment of the court. Their duty is to furnish the Judge or jury with the necessary scientific criteria for testing the accuracy of their conclusions so as to enable the application of their criteria to the facts proved in evidence. The scientific opinion, if intelligible, convincing and tested becomes a factor (and often an important factor) for consideration along with the whole other evidence in the case, but the decision is for the Judge and jury."

Expert Evidence and Opinion Evidence

Historically the courts have always striven to prevent any witness from expressing his opinion on an issue which the court has to decide. In *DPP v. Jordan* [1977] AC 699 Lord Wilberforce explained that it is for the jury to consider for themselves and reach their conclusions as to its effect.

"They cannot be told by psychologists or anyone else what the effects of the material (i.e. obscene publications) might be. The reason for this has sometimes been said to be in the supposed common law rule excluding direct evidence as to the ultimate issue to be decided, but I think that it (or this may be true of the rule itself) rests on a less technical basis, namely upon the principle that since the decision has been given to the jury as representing the ordinary man, it follows that, at any rate as matters affecting the ordinary man, the jury, as such, must make it."

Lord Wilberforce then pointed out that to this general rule there may be an exception in a case where the likely readers are a special class, such that a jury cannot be expected to understand the likely impact of the material upon its members without assistance. In such a case, evidence from persons qualified by study or experience of that class may be admissible.

Inroads on the Common-Law Rule: *"The expert may not usurp the function of the Court"*

The decision in *DPP v. AB and C Chewing Gum Ltd* (1968) 1 QB 159 may be regarded as making inroads into the common-law rule that an expert witness may not be asked questions which the court has to decide. Expert evidence was admitted as regards the likely impact of the material on children. In a prosecution under the Obscene Publications Act 1959, it was held that a child psychiatrist's evidence about the effect which 'battle cards' sold with packets of chewing gum would have on children of various ages from five upwards (whether the cards were likely to deprave and corrupt children) should have been admitted on the issue. In ordinary cases jurors and magistrates are as capable as anyone else of judging the likely effect of publication, but where children are concerned, "any jury and any justices need all the help they can get." Lord Parker LCJ observed, making the general point,

> "Those who practise in the criminal courts see every day cases of experts being called on the question of diminished responsibility, and although technically the final question 'Do you think he was suffering from diminished responsibility?' is strictly inadmissible, it is allowed time and time again without objection."

In *R. v. Stockwell* (1993) 97 CAR 260 the issue was taken further. Lord Taylor LCJ said that whether an expert can give an opinion on what has been called the ultimate issue, had long been a vexed question:

> "The rationale behind the supposed prohibition is that the expert should not usurp the functions of the jury. But since counsel can bring the witness so close to opining on the ultimate issue that the inference as to his view is obvious, the rule can only be ... a matter of form rather than substance. In our view an expert is called to give his opinion and he should be allowed to do so. It is, however, important that the Judge should make clear to the jury that they are not bound by the expert's opinion, and that the issue is for them to decide."

The Ultimate Issue: Criminal Cases

Commenting upon the recognition by the criminal law that

opinion evidence may be relevant even in questions of credibility, Lady Justice Butler-Sloss, in *Re M and R (Minors (Expert Opinion Evidence))* CA (1996) 2 FCR 617, said that 10 years ago such evidence would have been rejected but now:

> "It is possible to discern a more indulgent attitude (to the reception of expert evidence as to the defendant's mental state) in the Court of Appeal and in the practice of Judges in the Crown Court" (Archbold 1995 4.339).

In *R. v. Brien and Others* (CA Criminal Division) (2000) *The Times*, February 16, Lord Justice Roch LJ said that it was now accepted that expert evidence was admissible if it demonstrates some form of abnormality relevant to the reliability of a defendant's confession or evidence. The real criterion must be whether the abnormal disorder might render the confession or evidence unreliable. There should be a history pre-dating the making of admissions or giving evidence which was not based solely on a history given by the subject, and which pointed to or explained the abnormality or abnormalities. Furthermore, if such evidence was admitted the jury must be directed that they were not obliged to accept such evidence.

The Ultimate Issue: Civil Cases

In a civil case it is the Judge's duty to decide, and only the Judge, whether a witness should be believed. In *Re N (A Minor) Child Abuse: Evidence* (1996) 2 FCR 572 the limitations of expert's role in interpreting video evidence were defined by Ward LJ. He said that a Judge approaching a video of a child's interview should remind himself that the recording is admitted as a form of hearsay. It is for the Judge to decide its weight and credibility. Expert evidence would be received to explain and interpret the video. Such evidence would cover such things as the nuances of emotion and behaviour.

Although this was a family law case, Ward LJ's summary of the position is apposite to all civil cases:

> "(i) The expert's evidence of his or her belief in the truth of what the child is saying is ordinarily inadmissible because it trespasses upon the Judge's domain and usurps his functions.
>
> (ii) Proper evidence from an expert will be couched in terms that fact (a) or (b) is consistent with or inconsistent with sexual abuse, that it renders the child's evidence capable or incapable of being accepted by the Judge as true."

As Lady Justice Butler Sloss emphasised in *Re M and R (Minors) (Expert Opinion: Evidence)* (1996) 2 FCR 617 the Judge must never lose sight of the central truth: namely that the ultimate decision is for him and that all questions of relevance and weight are for him. "The modern view is to regard such matters by way of weight, rather than admissibility."

Developments in the Law and in Expertise

The law is always developing and has, among other things, to deal with new fields of expertise. In *R. v. Robb* (1991) 93 CAR 161 evidence of voice identification given by an expert witness, who was well qualified by academic training and practical experience to express an opinion, was held by the Court of

Appeal to be admissible even where the expert relied solely on a technique which was accepted by the majority of professional opinion to be unreliable unless supplemented by acoustic analysis. The facts of the case were that Dr. Dalloul, a wealthy Middle Eastern businessman, was kidnapped and held in a cottage in Kent. Demands for his ransom were telephoned to his wife: the calls were tape recorded. The appellant was charged with involvement in the kidnapping, and the allegation was that it was he who telephoned the ransom demand to Mrs. Dalloul. At the appellant's flat a video tape with his voice on it was found. The Crown sought to rely on an expert witness who gave his opinion that the voice on the demand for ransom tapes and the video tapes was the same. The defence sought, unsuccessfully, to have the tapes excluded. The Judge had directed the jury that the function of the expert was "to provide the court - that is you, the jury - with possible scientific reasons to allow you to form your opinion and judgment in relation to the matters that you find proved to your satisfaction. Remember, no expert can usurp your function as the final arbiter of fact. He is available to assist you with his experience." Bingham LJ in giving the judgment of the Court of Appeal said that their Lordships regarded that as a sound statement of legal principle. The witness was a phonetician who was well qualified by academic training and practical experience to express an opinion on voice identification.

Another example is *R. v. Toner* (1991) 93 CAR 361 where the Court of Appeal held that the possible effect of hypoglycaemia on the intent of the appellant in a case of attempted murder and wounding with intent to commit grievous bodily harm was outside the ordinary experience of jurors, who could not bring to bear their own judgment without the assistance of expert evidence. The trial Judge had ruled that the appellant's counsel was not permitted in re-examination to question a doctor about the effect a mild hypoglycaemia attack might have, so as to negative the appellant's specific intent, which the prosecution had to establish. However, the Court of Appeal was of the view that without expert evidence as to the effect, if any, that mild hypoglycaemia might have upon a man's ability to form an intent, the jury were deprived of assistance in a field where their ordinary experience did not enable them to judge for themselves. Despite the careful summing up of all other issues, the verdicts had to be regarded as unsound and unsafe, and a retrial was ordered.

It is of course questionable as to the amount of reliance which should be placed on the opinion if the expert has been unable to thoroughly investigate the matter, eg, to determine whether a man died of any particular disease. The symptoms having been proved, a physician may be called to give in evidence his opinion of the disease of which the man died. This evidence of opinion may be given, although the physician had never seen the deceased, as founded upon the symptoms. In *R. v. Mason* [1911] 7 Cr App R 67, a trial for murder, wounds and condition having been described, a surgeon was called upon to give in evidence his opinion as to whether the deceased died of his wounds from natural causes or whether the wounds were self-inflicted. The ultimate issue was, of course, for the jury to decide, having heard all the evidence in the case.

CHAPTER 2

Access to Justice Report

"Justice, I think, is the tolerable accommodation of the conflicting interests of society."
Learned Hand 1872-1961

In recent years there has been growing unease amongst the Judiciary concerning the changing role of expert witnesses brought about principally by the ever increasing emphasis on commercial considerations at the expense, very often, of strict professional conduct. As a result in 1994 a committee chaired by Lord Woolf was appointed to make recommendations that would improve access to justice and reduce costs of litigation.

The Woolf Recommendations for Reform

In their report, "Access to Justice" (1996), Lord Woolf MR and his committee recommended sweeping changes to the rules which govern civil litigation in England and Wales.

The subject of the expert witness figured prominently throughout the consultative process. It caused the committee great concern:

"The comments were not confined to specific classes of litigation. While the criticisms differed in detail depending on the type of proceedings which were being considered, the general thrust was the same. The need to engage experts was a source of excessive expense, delay and, in some cases, increased complexity through the excessive or inappropriate use of experts. Concern was also expressed as to their failure to maintain their independence from the party by whom they had been instructed." (*Access to Justice*, Section V, Chapter 23).

The Civil Procedure Rules 1998

The recommendations of *Access to Justice* were put into force by the Civil Procedure Rules 1998. The Rules apply to all civil proceedings. Their overriding objective is to enable the court to deal with all cases justly. In *Baron v. Lovell* (1999) *The Times*, September 14 (CA) Lord Woolf said that a main purpose of the Rules was to encourage parties to act co-operatively in the conduct of proceedings. The Rules are specific, eg, R35, "Expert evidence shall be restricted to that which is reasonably required to resolve the proceedings."

Definition of an Expert

An "expert" in the context of the Rules is a reference to an expert who has been instructed to give or prepare evidence for the purpose of court proceedings (R35.2). No party may call an expert or put in evidence an expert's report without the court's permission (R35.4[1]).

A party to a dispute is entitled to appoint an expert to advise or assist them on any particular issue. This advisory expert is sometimes known as a "shadow expert". The appointment can be made without seeking permission of the court and without divulging the contents of the report to the other side. In some complicated cases involving technical matters a barrister, before drafting the statement of claim, will request his instructing solicitor for the benefit of a shadow expert's advice and assistance.

The Overriding Duty of an Expert Witness

The overriding duty of an expert witness is clearly set out in the Civil Procedure Rules 1998. By Rule 35.3:

(1) It is the duty of an expert witness to help the court on matters within his expertise.

(2) This duty overrides any obligations to the person from whom he has received instructions or by whom he is paid.

This conception is not new. Over the years the courts have expressed their views in no uncertain terms. In *Whitehouse v. Jordan* both the Court of Appeal and the House of Lords dealt with the matter in terms of some scathing detail. That was a case in which the claimant who was born with severe brain damage, claimed this had been caused by the professional negligence of the senior registrar of the hospital at the time of birth. The Court of Appeal and then the House of Lords held that the evidence was not of sufficient strength to lead to a finding of professional negligence.

In the Court of Appeal (1980) 1 All ER 65 referring to the report of two experts, Lord Denning said:

"In the first place, their joint report suffers to my mind from the way it was prepared. It was the result of long conferences between two professors and counsel in London, and was actually 'settled' by counsel. In short, it wears the colours of special pleading rather than an impartial report. Whenever counsel 'settle' documents we know how it goes. 'We had better put this in.' 'We had better leave this out,' and so forth. A striking instance is the way in which Professor Tizard's was 'doctored'. The lawyers blocked out a couple of lines in which he agreed with Professor Strang that there was no negligence."

In the House of Lords (1981) 1 WLR 246, having dealt with the issue in the case, Lord Wilberforce said:

"One final word. I have to say I feel some concern as to the manner in which part of the expert evidence called for the plaintiff came to be organized. The matter was discussed in the Court of Appeal and commented on by Lord Denning. While some degree of consultation between experts and legal advisers is entirely proper, it is necessary that expert evidence presented to the court should be, and should be seen to be, the independent product of the expert, uninfluenced as to the form or contents by the exigencies of litigation. To the extent that it is not, the evidence is likely to be not only incorrect but self-defeating."

Duties and Responsibilities of the Expert Witness

In *National Justice Compania Naviera S.A. v. Prudential Assurance Company Ltd (Ikarian Reefer)* (1993) 2 Lloyds Rep 88, a fire broke out in the engine room of a ship and the owners sued for what they claimed was an insurable loss. The underwriters' defence was that the Ikarian Reefer had been deliberately set on fire with the owners' connivance. The question was whether this was proved to the required standard, and an expert was called.

Mr Justice Cresswell held that the duties and responsibilities of expert witnesses in civil cases included the following:

(a) Expert evidence presented to the court should be, and should be seen to be, the independent product of the expert uninfluenced as to the form or content by the exigencies of litigation.

(b) An expert witness should provide independent assistance to the court by way of objective unbiased opinion in relation to matters within his expertise.

(c) An expert witness should state the facts or assumptions upon which his opinion is based. He should not omit to consider material facts which could detract from his concluded opinion.

(d) An expert should make it clear when a question or issue fell outside his expertise.

(e) If the opinion was not properly researched because it was considered that insufficient data was available, then that had to be stated with an indication that the opinion was provisional. If the witness could not assert that the report contained the truth, the whole truth and nothing but the truth, then the qualification should be stated in the report.

(f) If, after exchange of reports, an expert witness changed his mind on a material matter, then the change of view should be communicated to the other side through legal representatives without delay, and when appropriate to the court.

(g) Photographs, plans, survey reports and other documents referred to in the expert evidence have to be provided to the other side at the same time as the exchange of the reports.

In *Stevens v. Gullis* (1999) *The Times*, October 6, 1999 (CA) Lord Woolf MR said that in the above case Mr Justice Cresswell had summarised the duties of an expert witness. Those requirements had been underlined by the 1998 Rules and it was now clear from them that in addition to the duty owed to the party who instructed him the expert witness was also under an overriding duty to the court.

Lord Woolf has since stressed that R35.3 shifts the focus from the client to the court with the intention of achieving impartiality. (John Bolton Memorial Lecture. "The Independent Expert". *Academy of Experts*. February 22, 2000).

CHAPTER 3

Appointment of Experts

"Let independence be our boast,
Ever mindful what it cost."

James Hopkinson (1770-1842)

The preliminary stages of litigation usually commence when the lay client contacts a solicitor and receives some advice. On receiving instructions from the lay client the solicitor will no doubt make preliminary investigations and advise the client on the necessity or otherwise of seeking expert advice. The solicitor may write a 'letter before action' to the prospective defendant, setting out the general nature of the allegations. The prospective defendant in his turn will probably contact a solicitor.

Negotiations can take place between the solicitors at any stage and it is more than likely that the case will be compromised on terms agreed by the parties. An advisory report by an expert is likely to assist the solicitor in assessing the strength of the case and in forming the advice he gives to the lay client concerning the possible terms of the settlement.

The Expert Adviser

The general rule is that any communications, whether oral, by letter or in the form of any documents passing between a legal adviser and an expert adviser (sometimes known as a "shadow expert") retained to make a report and offering advice, cannot be disclosed in legal proceedings without the consent of the client. The client can waive the privilege, the lawyer cannot. The position of the expert adviser comes within the extension of that rule. The reason for the rule is that it would not be possible to conduct legal affairs unless there can be free and frank discussion between a legal adviser and his client.

In *Waugh v. British Railway Board* (1980) AC 521 Lord Wilberforce said, "Everything should be done in order to encourage anyone who knows the facts to state them fully and candidly. As Sir George Jessel MP said, 'to bare his breast to his lawyer' (*Anderson v. Bank of British Columbia* (1876) 2 Ch 844). This he may not do unless he knows that his communication is privileged."

Party Appointed Expert Witness

If it is intended that the expert, whether or not he has earlier acted as an adviser, should be instructed to prepare a written report for the purpose of court proceedings, he is subject to the control of the court and the Civil Procedures Rules 1998 apply.

If the expert has already acted as an adviser, it would be prudent for the solicitor to issue fresh instructions to him, in writing, appointing him as an expert witness.

Rule 35.4 states that no party may call an expert or put in evidence an expert's report without the court's permission. Thus if he is instructed to give or prepare evidence, the expert will know that the court's permission has been granted, and that the court has decided that expert evidence was reasonably required to resolve the proceedings.

Importance of the Report of the Expert Witness

The court has wide powers to exercise control of case management and there is a general requirement (R35.5(i)) that expert evidence is to be given in a written report unless the courts direct otherwise. This means that in the majority of cases in which he is involved, the expert will not give oral evidence in the witness box unless he is called by the other party for cross-examination. We deal more fully with the contents of the expert's report in Chapter 4.

Lord Woolf's Contribution to Reform

In *Access to Justice* (1996) Lord Woolf and his committee recognized that an excessive use of experts by the parties causes delay and inflates litigation costs as well as encouraging partiality on the part of the experts. Lord Woolf stated intention was:

> "To try, from the start, to foster an approach which emphasizes the expert's duty to help the court impartially on matters within his expertise, and encourage a more focused use of expert evidence by a variety of means."

Some experts who, in the past, have been described as "claimants experts" or "defendant's experts" will find that the parties to the litigation while accepting that a single joint expert would be a proper appointment in a particular case, cannot agree on a particular person being selected.

We predict that there will be a considerable drop in income of some former experts who, not having functioned in their primary professional field for some time, hold themselves out as "professional expert witnesses" who can be relied upon by one party only, eg, in a personal injury case by the claimant, or by the defendant company's insurers.

Single Joint Expert

The court now has power to direct that evidence is to be given by a single joint expert. This is done at a pre-trial review when two or more parties wish to submit expert evidence on a particular issue (Civil Procedure Rules 1998 R35.7).

Where the parties cannot agree who the expert should be, the court cannot select the single joint expert, but it may:

1. select the expert from a list prepared or identified by the parties; or
2. direct that the expert be selected in such other manner as the court may direct (R35.8).

Certainly the Family Division intends to make full use of this power. The President, in a Practice Direction (ancillary relief procedure) (2000) 2 FCR 216, stated that as the introduction of expert evidence is likely to increase costs considerably the court will use its powers to restrict the unnecessary use of experts. Accordingly where expert evidence is sought to be relied upon, the parties should, if possible, agree upon a single joint expert whom they can jointly instruct. "Where parties are unable to agree upon the expert to be instructed the court will consider using its powers under Pt 35 of the Civil Procedure Rules 1998 SI 1998/3132 to direct that evidence be given by one expert only."

The court may give directions concerning

(a)   the payment of the expert's fees and expenses; and

(b)   any instruction, examination or experiments which the expert wishes to carry out.

A number of experts who have undergone the bruising experience of what they perceive as prolonged, unnecessary and unfair cross-examination may prefer to be a single joint expert rather than a party appointed expert. They would still be subject to cross-examination - by both parties - but they can perceive themselves as being regarded as having a position of independence and neutrality. Their professional integrity would not be liable to attack every time they entered the witness box; and they would be able to devote all their energy to giving independent evidence, without having to be very wary of a hostile foray from counsel to one of the parties.

As with a party appointed expert witness, the single joint expert has an overriding duty to the court. No communication with any of the parties is privileged, and neither are his instructions from the parties nor his report to the court. If he gives evidence in the witness box he has immunity from any civil action as do all other witnesses.

CHAPTER 4

The Written Report of the Expert Witness

"Make that recollection as durable as possible by putting it down in writing."
Benjamin Franklin 1706-1790

The written report of the expert witness assumes an importance which stems from the *Access to Justice* Report and the court's determination to control the evidence of the expert witness.

Court's Power to Restrict Expert Evidence

The Civil Procedure Rules 1998 are specific. Rule 35.4:

    (1)   No party may call an expert or put in evidence an expert's report without the court's permission.
    (2)   When a party applies for permission under this rule he must identify:
        (a) the field in which he wishes to rely on expert evidence; and
        (b) where practical the expert in that field on whose evidence he wishes to rely.

Rule 35.5 states that evidence is to be given in a written report unless the court directs otherwise.

Appointment as an Expert Witness

Whichever method of appointment is used (see Chapter 3) the expert witness owes an overriding duty to the court, and his report must be addressed to the court. The individual concerned must be fully satisfied that he can answer all the following questions in the affirmative before proceeding:

1. Is the matter in dispute within his professional knowledge experience and competence? This is not always as straightforward as may appear in the first flush of enthusiasm, and some hard thinking may be necessary before reaching a decision, not only to do justice to the client's case, but also to his own professional reputation. Even if the expert feels able to accept instructions he may still have to decide whether, over and beyond his role, other disciplines should be involved and additional experts appointed to deal with other technical issues.

2. Is the expert unencumbered by any personal matters in accepting instructions? It hardly needs repeating that the expert witness must be impartial and any potential financial benefits (other than specific remunerations) either directly or indirectly must immediately rule out any involvement on the part of the expert. Further, there may be other disqualifying factors of a personal nature, eg, a family relationship. The first case in which one of the co-authors appeared was a landlord and tenant matter when one of his senior partners asked him to appear at short notice on behalf of the landlord, as an expert witness. Co-author, young and totally inexperienced, was puzzled and slightly resentful that he had been pressed into service.

The landlord was in fact an uncle of the senior partner concerned and it would therefore have been improper for him to act, as this had not been disclosed to the other side.

3. Is his evidence likely to help the court? The expert should not accept instructions if it is clear even from a cursory look at the papers that he cannot offer help.

4. Can he meet the time scale? This may seem obvious, but in practice may involve not only some calculations as to the future commitments already accepted, but also use of a crystal ball. For example, are there likely to be any obligations that may arise in the intervening period for a major client? Are any partners going to be away on holiday during this time, involving the potential expert witness in carrying some of their workload?

In *Matthews v. Tarmac Bricks and Tiles Ltd* (1999) *The Times,* July 1, Lord Woolf MR said that ways had to be found to meet the obvious requirement that cases should be heard expeditiously. He emphasised that doctors who held themselves out as practising in the medico-legal field had to be prepared to arrange their affairs to meet the commitments of the courts where that was practical.

The potential expert witness should not be beguiled into thinking that because in perhaps 95% of all the previous cases in which he was appointed an expert, a written report had been sufficient by way of evidence this will happen again. It may be the one case in which he will be required to give oral evidence as well. In *Rollinson v. Kimberley Clark Ltd* (1999) *The Times,* June 22, the Court of Appeal held that it was not acceptable when a trial date was fairly imminent for a solicitor to seek to instruct an expert without checking the availability of that expert for trial. If the solicitor did carry out the check and there was no reasonable prospect of securing his attendance for a year then the solicitor should instruct another expert.

Writing the Report

When preparing his report for the court the expert witness must at all times bear in mind:

(1) It is his duty to help the court on matters within his expertise; and

(2) This duty overrides any obligations to the person from whom he received his instructions (Civil Procedure Rules 1998 R35.1).

The report should be written in simple language in such a way that it can be understood by a layman. Whatever size paper is used it is important that there are wide margins on each side so that counsel and the Judges can make notes. We recommend that the report is labelled with a reference number: commonly the initials of the expert are used, eg, for Gordon David Smith GDS1, and that all paragraphs are numbered. The exhibits should then be labelled in the same fashion, ie, GDS2, GDS3 etc, in the same sequence as they are referred to in the report.

Scott Schedules

An integral element in a case of any magnitude is likely to be a Scott Schedule (first formulated by an Official Referee of that name in 1920). One party is required to list out in detail each item of his claim and the estimated cost, against which the other party sets out his views of the principle and finance involved. The final part of the schedule is left for the Judge to insert his comments and awards. The purpose is, of course, to save time at the hearing, although frequently the schedule will form the basis of agreement at the preliminary meeting.

Form of the Report

The Report must:

1. give details of the expert's qualifications;
2. give details of any literature or other material which the expert relied on in making his report;
3. state who carried out the test or experiment which the expert used or referred to, and whether or not the test or experiment had been carried out under the expert's supervision;
4. give the qualifications of the person who carried out such test or experiment;
5. where there is a range of opinion on the matter dealt with in the report:
   (a)summarise the range of opinion and
   (b)give reasons for his own opinion;
6. contain a summary of the range of the conclusions reached;
7. contain a statement that the expert understands his duty to the court and has complied with that duty (R35.10(1));
8. set out the substance of all material instructions, whether written or oral, on the basis of which the report was written.

Expert's Declaration

The expert's report for the court must be verified by a statement of truth as follows:

1. I understand that my duty in providing written reports and in giving evidence is to help the court and that this duty overrides any obligation to the party who has engaged me. I confirm that I have complied with my duty.
2. I believe that the facts I have stated in this report are true and the opinions I have expressed are correct.

The report must be signed by the expert.

In Appendix II we reproduce a model form of an expert witness's report.

Exhibits

"One picture is worth more than 10,000 words."
                                        (Ancient Chinese proverb)

The exhibits to be prepared comprise any artefact likely to be of assistance to the court. The most common are maps, plans, photographs and - increasingly - cassettes or videotapes. We would stress that so far as is humanly possible, all exhibits should be agreed between the parties beforehand. Few things are so irritating to Judges as, for example, two maps prepared by each side purporting to show the same area, but drawn to different scales and possibly even from different viewpoints.

Maps and Plans: Maps should invariably be produced with north at the top, but should always contain in addition a north point, and the scale should be clearly marked. A very common mistake is to produce maps that are too large, and hence difficult to handle. It is well worthwhile taking some time and effort to ensure that these are manageable. Further, never roll a map, unless this is absolutely unavoidable. Fold the map into rectangles of about A4 size, if at all possible, and in such a way that the reference number is always visible. We recall the French general who inquired why it was battles always took place at the very point where his map was folded.

Plans must also clearly indicate the scale, usually in the form, eg, "1:100" or alternatively "1/8th of an inch = 1 foot". Do not be apprehensive of expressing the scale as an approximation in those cases where a plan to a high degree of accuracy is not required. Frequently, for example, a single-line plan of a building will be perfectly sufficient to demonstrate the point(s) you wish to make.

Photographs: An important point to bear in mind is that if the photographs are not agreed, each and every photograph may have to be strictly proved, ie, the photographer will have to go into the witness box.

There should be one set only of the photographs, all of the same size, of the same finish, eg, matt or gloss, and all should carry a small inscription giving a concise and neutral description of the subject, the date the photograph was taken, and also (where appropriate) the time. Further, they should be accompanied by a map or plan showing the angle of view of each shot, these being numbered to correspond with those shown on the individual photographs.

Identification: Every exhibit, of whatever nature, must be identified with a number, or letter, or combination of the two. The most usual method of marking is by the expert's initials, ie, "GDS (GDS for Gordon David Smith) 1, 2, 3" etc.

A practical tip to simplify and speed up the process of identification is the use of small adhesive labels. These are now available in a great variety of sizes, shapes and colours and can be particularly helpful in preparing the inscriptions for photographs.

The exhibits must be numbered in the chronological order in which reference is made to them in the expert's report. It is a matter of choice whether to tender the exhibits as and when they are referred to when giving evidence, or - in our view the better alternative - to put them together in one "bundle" and to hand this to the tribunal and to the other party, when entering the witness box. There is a possible danger in the former method that the expert may lose some of his concentration if he has to stop and distribute exhibits every few minutes. Also it is very easy, in the stress of the occasion, to get them out of order. On the other hand, if they are all fitted together, it may be difficult for the Judge to make comparisons between one part and another. The most common method of fixing documents together nowadays is by punching holes in the top left-hand corner of each page, threading them together with cords having tabs at each end, and then - if you have one exhibit running to a number of pages - staple these together so that they can be extracted from the whole bundle as one unit.

It is sometimes necessary to bring many documents into court. If the intention is to refer to one page of a book, for example, it is perfectly acceptable to photocopy that one page in assembling the exhibits. However, remember to bring the original volume into court. The other aspect of this situation to be borne in mind is that if you quote from an acknowledged textbook, and it is accepted by the other side, then that becomes part of your evidence and is treated as such. Finally, any effort that is made to render the presentation of your exhibits as clear and straightforward as possible will be amply rewarded. Not only is this likely to make your evidence more acceptable to the court, but it gives greater confidence in the presentation.

Cross-referencing can be of vital importance in a complex case, where there may well be literally hundreds of exhibits.

CHAPTER 5

Outline of Civil Proceedings

"Liberty exists in proportion to wholesome restraint."
Daniel Webster 1782-1852
Speech at the Charleston Bar Dinner May 10, 1847

The Basis of Litigation

In *Davies v. Eli Lilly and Co.* (1987) 1 WLR 428, Lord Donaldson MR commented:

> "Litigation in this country is conducted 'cards upon the table'. Some people from other lands regard this as incomprehensible. 'Why,' they ask, 'should I be expected to provide my opponent with the means of defeating me?' The answer of course, is that litigation is not a war or even a game. It is designed to do real justice between opposing parties and, if the court does not have all the relevant information, it cannot achieve this object."

The Civil Procedure Rules 1998 apply to all proceedings: ie,

(a)   County Courts;
(b)   the High Court; and
(c)   the Civil Division of the Court of Appeal.

Other enactments deal with family proceedings (Matrimonial and Family Proceedings Act 1984, s.40) and adoption (Adoption Act 1976). Their overriding objective is to enable the court to deal with all cases justly. They follow the Access to Justice Report 1996. In *Baron v. Lovell* (1999) *The Times*, September 14, Lord Woolf MR said that the main purpose of the Rules was to encourage parties to act co-operatively in the conduct of proceedings.

Sequence of Proceedings

Statement of Claim
Proceedings begin with a Statement of Claim in the High Court or a county court, verified by a Statement of Truth. The Statement of Claim includes a claim form and particulars of the claim, including a concise statement of the facts on which the claimant relies. This is filed with a court and a copy served on the defendant.

Defence
A defendant wishing to defend must file a defence, which must state:

1. which of the allegations in the particulars of claim he denies;
2. which he is unable to admit or deny but requires the claimant to prove and
3. which he admits.

When he denies an allegation he must state his reasons for doing so and state his own version of events if it is different from that of the claimant. He may also add a counterclaim. This is all filed with the court and verified by a Statement of Truth.

Counterclaim
The claimant must file a defence to the counterclaim if this is in dispute.

Amendment
This is not as easy as it once was. When proceedings have been served, permission of the court is required for any amendment.

Further Information
A party may apply for further information, and the court may order a party to clarify any matter in dispute or give any additional information to any matter. This also must be verified by a Statement of Truth.

Categories of Cases

The county courts deal with about 90 per cent of all civil cases each year, although many construction industry cases will be heard in the Technology and Construction Court in the High Court. Any proceedings in contract or tort (eg, negligence) may be started in a county court. Certain claims must be started there - eg, personal injuries not exceeding £50,000.

Under the Civil Procedures Rules 1998, cases are divided into the following categories:

1. Small claims in the County Court, ie, less than £5,000. These are automatically referred to the District Judge for arbitration. The informal procedure is held in chambers. It

is unlikely that an expert witness will be involved, as only limited costs can be awarded.

2. Fast track cases. This is the normal track for any claim:

   (1) for which the small claim track is not the normal track;
   (2) the financial value of the claim is not more than £15,000;
   (3) the court considers that the trial is likely to last for no longer than one day;
   (4) oral expert evidence will be limited to one expert per party in relation to any expert field and the expert evidence will be limited to two expert fields.

3. Multi-track for cases over £15,000.
   Cases are allocated to one of these tracks depending on their value and complexity.

Active Case Management by the Court

Active case management by the court is an integral part of the new system. Case management conferences are usually only ordered when the case is a particularly complicated one, or where the action has suffered from neglect by the parties.

Insurance companies, among other interested parties, have on the whole welcomed

   (a) "front loading", ie, "aces on the table" at an early stage and
   (b) attendance by an insurance company's representative

together with the solicitor responsible for the case together with the claimant.

These have helped to clarify the issues and frequently lead to an early settlement.

Pre-Trial Review

On a day fixed for a pre-trial review of an action or matter, the Master (in the High Court), or the District Judge considers the course of the proceedings and gives such directions as appear to be necessary or desirable for securing the just, expeditious and economical disposal of the action or matter.

At the pre-trial review the Court directs every party to serve on the other parties written statements which the party intends to adduce on any issue of fact to be dealt with at the trial. This Rule, introduced in 1992, provided for the compulsory exchange of witness statements in County Courts. The object is to save time and expense at the trial by dispensing with the calling of witnesses, whether expert or not, where there is no dispute between the parties on the evidence, and to ensure that the parties are not taken by surprise.

The report, which the expert will use as the basis of his evidence at the trial, must be disclosed at this stage. The substance of the report which is relied on must be disclosed, and it is not acceptable for the expert to edit out a part of the report which does not favour his client. The disclosure includes any relevant matters contained in any letter covering the report.

Disclosure

At the pre-trial review, the Master/District Judge may order a party to disclose to the other parties in the action the documents which he has or has had under his control:

1. upon which he relies;
2. which adversely affect his own case; or
3. another party's case; or
4. which support any other party's case.

Disclosure is not automatic and in its case management the court controls the extent of the disclosure.

Meeting of Experts

A meeting of experts will normally be ordered by the Master/District Judge, before the trial. However, the court may, at any stage, direct a discussion between experts. This is usually done after the exchange of reports. The purpose is to identify the issues between the parties and to allow them to reach some form of agreement where possible.

At or following their meeting(s) the experts should prepare a joint memorandum for the court, setting out the issues on which they agree, and those on which they hold differing opinions. The contents of the discussion between the experts may not be referred to at the trial unless the parties agree.

A Single Joint Expert

At the pre-trial review when two or more parties wish to submit expert evidence on a particular issue the court may direct that the evidence is to be given by one expert only (Civil Procedures Rules 1998 R35.7).

We have dealt with elsewhere (Chapter 3) how the selection may be made.

Each party may give instructions to the expert but he must, at the same time, send a copy to the other party.

Although the court, ie, the District Judge, may take the view that in the particular case one expert is sufficient the parties do not always see it that way. One party may insist that the potential expert witness they wish to brief is essential to the case, while the other party is just as adamant that they too require another particular expert. In making his order for a single joint expert the District Judge is dependent upon the Circuit Judge and ultimately the Court of Appeal to uphold him.

CHAPTER 6

Outlines of Court Hearings

"The history of liberty has largely been the history of the
observation of procedural safeguards."
Felix Frankfurter *McNabb v. United States 1843*

A. Civil Court Hearings

Whether the trial takes place in the High Court or a county
court, the procedure is basically the same.

(a) Counsel for the claimant makes his opening speech
outlining the facts of the case to the Judge, reciting the
contentions of the parties, and indicating the areas of
dispute and those of agreement. Counsel (ie, a
barrister or a solicitor/advocate) will refer to any
relevant legal authorities. He will draw attention to any
agreed bundle of correspondence, documents, plans
or photographs. He will say whether or not, or to what
extent, the reports of the experts are agreed, or
whether the expert evidence is to be given by a single
joint expert.

Where counsel are agreed that the burden of proof
in the only matters of dispute rests on the defendant
the order of procedure can be altered and the case for
the defendant opened first.

(b) Counsel for the claimant calls his witnesses in a
consistent order, usually commencing with the

claimant. After taking the oath, the witness gives his evidence-in-chief. All that is necessary is for him to say that the contents of his statement are true. If there are matters which require further elucidation or relevant events have taken place after the date of the statement, he can give evidence of these matters. With prior disclosure of witness statements, the witness need not repeat the whole of his statement, ie, he may omit the facts that are not in contest (these matters will have been the subject of agreement between counsel). Questions asked of a witness by counsel who calls him should not be of a leading nature, but should bring out the evidence which the witness expected to give, ie, of what he saw, heard or did.

An expert witness is, of course, entitled to state his opinion on the issue in question, once the facts are elicited and his expertise established. One should bear in mind however that if his opinion is based on the wrong facts, the opinion will be flawed and of no assistance to the court.

(c)   Counsel for the defendant has the right to cross-examine the witness. Questions put in cross-examination must be either relevant and pertinent to the matter in issue, or calculated to attack the witness's claim to credibility. Unlike the examination-in-chief, counsel may ask leading questions, ie, ones which suggest what the answer will be.

Wigmore (Chadbourne Revision, 1974) suggests that:

"... it may be in more than one sense cross-examination takes the place in our system which torture occupied in the medieval system of civilians. Nevertheless, it is beyond any doubt the greatest legal machine ever invented for the discovery of truth. However difficult it may be for the layman, the scientist or the foreign jurist to appreciate its wonderful power, there has probably never been a moment's doubt upon this point in the mind of the lawyer of experience. 'You can do anything,' said Wendell Phillips, 'with a bayonet - except sit upon it.' A lawyer can do anything with cross-examination - if he is skilful enough not to impale his own cause upon it."

Wigmore goes on to explain that cross-examination brings out the undesirable facts of the case, modifying the examination-in-chief, or otherwise adding to the cross-examiner's own case.

(d)   Counsel for the claimant has the right to re-examine the witness on any matter which has been raised in cross-examination.

It is likely that the expert witness called on behalf of the claimant will give his evidence last, after the facts upon which he is going to give his opinion have been established. If the expert is a witness of fact as well as of opinion, it may not be necessary to call him last.

(e)   Counsel for the defendant, if he is calling evidence, opens his case to the Judge.

(f)   Witnesses for the defendant are called in a logical sequence, and are subject to examination-in-chief, cross-examination, and re-examination.

Again, the expert witness is likely to give his evidence last. If, however, the expert is giving professional evidence only, subject to agreement between counsel the expert called by the defendant can give that evidence directly following the expert called by the claimant. However, if the experts are testifying to fact as well as opinion, this course will not be possible.

(g)   Counsel for the defendant addresses the Judge on law and fact.

(h)   Counsel for the claimant addresses the Judge on law and fact.

(i)   The Judge gives his judgment. If the case has any complications, either of law or fact, the judgment is usually reserved to another date of hearing.

The Special Case of Care Proceedings

By the Children Act 1989, all care proceedings commence in the Family Proceedings Court, which is a specially constituted court of the magistrates' court. If the proceedings are estimated to be lengthy, or complicated, in either law or fact, they are likely to be transferred to the Family Hearing Centres, a specially constituted court of a county court. In particular cases, where for example a new and potentially difficult point of law arises, or there is an overseas element, this will be to the Family Division of the High Court.

Where the case is transferred to the High Court or a Family Hearing Centre, the hearing will follow a similar procedure to that of all civil trials, although there may be procedural difficulties because so many parties are involved. The case will always be heard by a single Judge.

If the case remains in the Family Proceedings Court, the bench will consist of three magistrates, with a legally qualified clerk. Counsel for the local authority, which brings the proceedings, will open his case and call witnesses. Counsel or solicitor for the parents (who may be separately represented) may cross-examine each witness, as may counsel or solicitor representing the child. The complicated sequence of procedure is fully set out in *Child Abuse Procedure and Evidence* (Graham Hall and Martin, 3rd Edition, 1992, Barry Rose).

It is worth bearing in mind that the cases in which experts are called to give evidence are likely to be transferred for hearing to the Family Hearing Centres, and will therefore follow the basic outline described in civil hearings.

B. Criminal Court Hearings

All proceedings in criminal matters commence in the magistrates' court for the area in which the offence is alleged to have occurred. The vast majority of cases end there because:

(i)   the offence is one which can only be tried summarily; or

(ii)   although the offence is triable either way, the prosecution and the defence make representations that the case should be tried summarily and the court agrees.

(a) Committal proceedings - where applicable
Cases which may be triable either way are first subject to committal proceedings in the magistrates' court for the area in which the alleged offence occurred. Sitting as examining justices, the court considers the evidence put forward by the prosecution. The examining magistrate(s) must consider the evidence but the Criminal Procedure and Investigation Act 1996

47

removed the necessity of live witnesses. On the basis of written evidence the court makes its decision as to whether there is a case to answer. An expert who will be called by the prosecution at the trial is not, therefore, required to attend the committal proceedings.

The defence has the opportunity to make a submission of no case to answer. The standard of proof required from the prosecution at this stage is low, but if the defence succeeds the accused will be discharged. This is not the same as an acquittal and the prosecution, having gathered further evidence, may seek to commit the accused for a second time.

Cases which must be tried by a jury, ie, indictable only, are subject to Section 51(1) of the Crime and Disorder Act 1998, which came into effect on January 15, 2001. Committal proceedings are abolished and the cases are sent forthwith from the magistrates' court to the Crown Court. All proceedings preliminary to trial are dealt with there.

(b) Trial in the magistrates' court
(a) The Bench consists of either a District Judge (magistrates' court) or three lay magistrates. The prosecuting authority outlines the basic elements of the case, dealing with the law and the facts which must be proved, and then calls the witnesses in a logical sequence. Each is subject to examination-in-chief, cross-examination and re-examination. An expert called by the prosecution is likely to be called last and may have to remain outside the court until other evidence is complete. An expert to be called by the defence, if not also giving evidence of fact, should be allowed to be present in court while this evidence is given.

(b)   Counsel (barrister or solicitor) for the defence may submit that there is no case in law to answer. Counsel for the prosecution must then be permitted to be heard on this issue. If the submission succeeds the trial is at an end. If not, the case for the defence begins.

(c)   Counsel for the defence must choose between making an opening speech or a closing one. The defendant and any witnesses then give their evidence according to the same procedure as that applicable to the prosecution.

(d)   The bench then announces its decision. Usually a lay bench retires before doing this. If the accused is found guilty, the bench proceeds to sentence.

(e)   An appeal from the decision of the magistrates' court lies to the Crown Court on law and/or fact, or to the Divisional Court of the High Court on law only. At the Crown Court the bench will consist of a Judge and lay justices. The proceedings start *de novo*, ie, in exactly the same sequence as in the magistrates' court. Each side may decide to call witnesses other than those called in the magistrates' court.

A word of warning to experts giving evidence in a trial at the magistrates' court and then called to give evidence in the Crown Court: ie, although there is no official court record of the evidence given in the magistrates' court, it is likely that a legal clerk for one of the parties will have taken a note. The expert in cross-examination should expect the question:

"In the proceedings in the magistrate's court did you not say...?"
Appropriate answer: "That is not a correct record of what I

said", or "Yes" - and give an explanation.

(c) Trial by Jury in the Crown Court
  (a)   The defendant will be arraigned, ie, the charge(s) read to him by the clerk of the court.
  (b)   f the defendant pleads guilty, he will be sentenced by the Judge.
  (c)   If the defendant pleads not guilty, the jury will be empanelled, ie, 12 men and women sworn, or by affirmation if the juror so requests, to try the case according to the evidence.
  (d)   If there is an application by counsel either for the prosecution or the defence on any preliminary points of law to be decided, or an application for the exclusion of certain potential evidence, this will be done in the absence of the jury.
  (e)   Opening of the Crown case by counsel for the prosecution, outlining the basic elements of law which the Crown has to prove, and the evidence on which they intend to rely. Counsel will give preliminary guidance on the burden of proof, which lies with the Crown, and remind the jury that all points of law are ultimately matters for the Judge.
  (f)   Witnesses called for the Crown will each give their evidence, so far as possible in a sequence which "tells the story in a consistent manner". After giving his evidence-in-chief, each witness will be subject to cross-examination by counsel on behalf of each defendant and then if necessary, will be re-examined on any matter which arose in cross-examination by counsel for the Crown.
  (g)   If solicitors on behalf of each defendant have given

notice that they will not require that witness to be present as his evidence is not contested, then the evidence can be read, and that evidence is as much part of the case as if the witness had given evidence on oath in the witness box. This procedure saves time and money as well as dispensing with the attendance at court of the witness, as in civil trials.

The expert witness is likely to be the last of the witnesses to be called, so that the facts, upon which he is going to express his opinion, have already been established. An expert who is to be called by the prosecution will already have made his report in writing, and this must be disclosed before trial, as must all other prosecution witness statements, to the defence.

The defence may later wish to call an expert witness but this cannot be done without leave of the Judge if the defence has not disclosed the expert's written report to the court prior to the trial (Crown Court [advance notice of expert evidence] Rules 1997).

The expert - and the same applies to any expert called on behalf of the defendant - will be permitted to remain in court until he gives his evidence, unless there is a successful application by defence counsel that he should remain outside the court until he is called to the witness box to give his evidence. To the authors' knowledge the tactic was first employed when Sir Bernard Spilsbury, who had built up a reputation of infallibility as an expert witness, was called to give evidence in the trial of Mrs Elvira Barney for the murder of Thomas Scott Stephen. Previously Sir Bernard had always been allowed to sit in the court throughout the trial and give his medical opinion on the evidence he had heard. To counteract this, Sir Patrick Hastings, QC, one of the most brilliant advocates of the 20th century, successfully applied on behalf of the defence to have Sir Bernard excluded from the court during the opening of the case and during the calling of the evidence.

The tactic was also employed by the defence in another trial for murder: *Abbott v. Port of Spain* [1977] AC 755, when Dr Keith Simpson was successfully excluded from the courtroom until the time came for him to give his evidence. However, the appeal against conviction to the Privy Council did not turn on this point, and the appeal was dismissed.

(h) At the end of the case for the Crown, counsel for the defence may, in the absence of the jury, make a submission to the Judge that the Crown has not proved all the elements of the offence with which the defendant is charged, and therefore there is no case for him to answer.

(i) If the submission is successful, the Judge will direct the jury to find the defendant "not guilty", and he is acquitted. Otherwise, the case continues.

(j) If the defence is calling other witnesses besides the defendant himself, counsel for the defence may make an opening speech to the jury, outlining the case for the defendant.

If only the defendant is to be called, it is usual for counsel to reserve his speech until after the defendant has been called. Unlike the prosecution, the defendant has the right, in those circumstances, to have only one speech made to the jury on his behalf.

(k)   If he is going to give evidence on his own behalf, the defendant gives his evidence first. He is subject, as are all witnesses, to cross-examination first on behalf of any co-defendant(s) and then by the Crown. Again, any expert witness called by a defendant is likely to be last in the sequence. Each defendant closes his case before the next defendant commences.

(l)   At the end of the evidence for the defence, counsel for the Crown makes his closing speech to the jury, followed by counsel for each defendant.

(m)   The Judge delivers his summing-up to the jury, directing them on points of law and summarizing the evidence.

(n)   The jury retires to consider its verdict. At this stage it must be unanimous. However, at any time after two hours have elapsed, depending upon the gravity and length of the case, the Judge can give a direction that he can accept the verdict of the jury, whatever the verdict be, so long as 10 of its 12 are agreed on their verdict.

(o)   The jury returns and delivers its verdict. If the verdict is "not guilty", the defendant is acquitted. If the verdict is "guilty", the Judge proceeds to sentence the defendant.

Criminal Courts Review

In December 1999 Lord Justice Auld was appointed by the Lord Chancellor to report on the working of the criminal courts. His terms of reference were:

> "A review into the practices and procedures of, and the rules of evidence applied by, the criminal courts at every level, with a view to ensuring that they deliver justice fairly, by streamlining all their processes, increasing their efficiency and strengthening the effectiveness of their relationships with others across the whole of the criminal justice system, and having regard to the interests of all parties including the victims and witnesses, thereby promoting public confidence in the rule of law."

Lord Justice Auld has welcomed information and views on a number of issues. Of particular interest to potential expert witnesses are:

(i)   case management, procedure and evidence;
(ii)   liaison between courts and agencies involved in the criminal system;
(iii)   management of the system.

Taking the Oath

The general common-law rule is that testimony of a witness at a trial is not admissible unless he has previously been sworn to tell the truth.

Section 1 of the Oaths Act 1978 lays down the procedure. The person taking the oath shall hold the New Testament, or in the case of a Jew, the Old Testament, in his uplifted hand and swear after the person duly authorized to administer oaths (e.g. the clerk of the tribunal, an usher of the court):

> "I swear by Almighty God that the evidence which I shall give shall be the truth, the whole truth and nothing but the truth".

If the witness is neither a Christian nor Jew, but not agnostic, nor wishing to affirm, he may swear on a relevant holy book (which the tribunal may or may not have available).

By s.5, any person who objects to being sworn shall be permitted to make his solemn affirmation instead of taking the oath. All that the witness who wishes to affirm - for whatever reason (e.g. an agnostic, or someone with an objection to taking an oath) - has to do is to say to the court: "May I affirm please?" Then he will make his affirmation as follows:

> "I (name) do solemnly, sincerely and truly declare and affirm that the evidence which I shall give shall be the truth, the whole truth and nothing but the truth."

We are aware how much it sometimes troubles a witness that he is not addressing the tribunal correctly, although this feeling is rarely reciprocated by the tribunal itself. One of the co-authors has been addressed as "Your Majesty", Your Highness", "Sir" (when it was fairly obvious it should have been "Madam") and even "Excuse Me". The correct modes of address are as follows:

Correct Mode of Address to the Court/Tribunal

High Court	My Lord, My Lady
Central Criminal Court	My Lord, My Lady
Other Crown Courts	Your Honour

County Court

Circuit Judge	Your Honour
District Judge	Sir/Madam

Magistrates' Court

District Judge	Sir/Madam
Chairman of Lay Bench	Sir/Madam

Coroner's Court	Sir/Madam

All Tribunals	Sir/Madam

CHAPTER 7

Rules of Evidence

*"People in general have no notion of the sort and amount of
evidence often needed to prove the simplest matter of fact."*
Peter Mere Latham (1789-1875): *Collected Works*

It is disturbing for an expert witness if he loses confidence in the
witness box simply because he is not sure what he may or may
not say. He is likely to be particularly fearful that counsel for the
other side will object to an important piece of evidence because
it is "hearsay". For this reason, we have devoted Chapter 8 to
the rules concerning "hearsay". In this chapter we will deal with
the other rules of evidence which the expert is likely to
encounter.

What is Evidence?

"Evidence is the usual means of proving or disproving a fact
in issue. The law of evidence indicates what may properly be
introduced by a party (that is, what is admissible) and also
what standard of proof is necessary in any particular case. In
short the law of evidence governs the means and manner in
which a party may substantiate his own case, or refute that
of his opponent." (Halsbury's *Laws of England* 4th Edn,
Vol.17).

The Burden of Proof

It is a basic principle that the party who brings the case must prove his contentions. This legal burden remains constant throughout the trial. If at the conclusion of the trial, he has failed to establish this, he will lose the case. The evidential burden may shift from one party to another during the trial, depending on the balance of evidence at a particular stage in the trial.

The party bearing the legal burden must satisfy the tribunal that a greater weight can be attached to evidence in his case than that of his opponent. "He who avers must prove" is an old adage of the courts. This is known as the standard of proof.

In civil cases the standard of proof is satisfied on the balance of probabilities. In criminal cases the standard required of the prosecution is beyond all reasonable doubt and the jury must be satisfied by the evidence so that they are sure that the prosecution has established the guilt of the defendant.

The Best Evidence Rule

Historically, the English courts have regarded the best evidence to be that of a person who observed what transpired, heard what was said/or acted in a particular manner, and is present in the court to describe this and be cross-examined upon it. Further, the best evidence of a document is production of the original, and the same applies to any article. However, there have been considerable inroads in this doctrine and there has been a gradual decline in its strict application to such an extent that some commentators regard the best evidence rule as virtually obsolete.

The effect of all that remains (ie, that if an original document is available to a party, that party must produce it and cannot give secondary evidence by producing a copy) is that if the party has the original of the document with him in court or could have the original in court without any difficulty, the court will infer the worst if he refuses to produce the original and can give no reasonable explanation. In *R. v. Governor of Pentonville Prison ex parte Osman* [1989] 3 All ER 701 Lloyd LJ commented: "This court would be more than happy to say goodbye to the best evidence rule."

Secondary Evidence

In the unavoidable absence of the best or primary evidence of documents, the court will accept secondary evidence. As explained in Halsbury (4th Edn. Vol.17), this is evidence which suggests, on the face of it, that other and better evidence exists. A party tendering it ought therefore to show that he is unable to obtain the best evidence. There are no degrees of secondary evidence, and once it has been shown that a private document cannot be produced for reasons which admit the giving of secondary evidence, the contents may be proved by any type of secondary evidence, eg, a copy which can be proved to have been correctly made from the original, a counterpart, or a draft, by a sworn oral testimony as to the contents of the original document.

Public and judicial documents are usually proved by copies, without explanation of the absence of the originals. The document must be available for public inspection.

Reliance on Other Expert Opinion

When the expert witness is asked to express his opinion on a question, the primary facts on which the opinion are based have to be proved by admissible evidence, given either by the expert himself or some other competent witness.

The co-authors cannot resist the temptation to insert a light-hearted note at this point. The story concerns a celebrated, and confident, expert witness who was about to be cross-examined. Counsel for the other party, wishing to lull the expert into a false sense of security opened fulsomely:

"I understand you are the leading authority in this country on ..."

E.W. (modestly): "Oh I don't know ...."

"And you are the author of what is generally regarded as the definitive work on the subject?"

E.W. (even more modestly): "Very kind of you to say so, but ..."

Counsel, going for the kill: "Then why is it that the opinion you have just expressed is completely contrary to what you say on p.589 of your book?"

E.W. (thoughtfully): "Ah, yes, I'm working on the Second Edition."

However, once the facts are proved, the expert is then entitled to draw on the work (including unpublished work) of others in his field of expertise as part of the process of arriving at his conclusion, provided he refers to that material in his evidence so that the cogency and probative value of his conclusion could be tested by reference to that material.

In *H. v. Schering Chemicals* [1983] 1 All ER 849 the documents included summaries of the result of research, articles and letters published in medical journals concerning drugs. Bingham, J said: "It is common ground, as I understand it, that these articles can be referred to for the purpose of showing the state of general professional knowledge which is of course relevant to the issue of what the defendants knew or ought to have known at any given time."

Reliance on the work of others does not infringe the hearsay rule. In *R. v. Abadom* [1983] 1 All ER 364, A was charged with robbery. At the trial the Crown's case rested on evidence that the appellant had broken a window during the robbery and fragments of glass which were found adhering to and embedded in a pair of shoes taken from A's home after his arrest had come from the window. An expert witness for the Crown gave evidence that he had consulted statistics completed by the Home Office Central Research Establishment and he found that the refractive index referred to occurred in only four per cent of all glass samples investigated by the establishment. He then gave his opinion that the glass from the shoes originated from the window. A was convicted and appealed, and contended that the evidence of the Home Office Research Establishment's statistics was hearsay and inadmissible because the expert witness had no personal knowledge of the analysis on which the statistics were based. The Court of Appeal held the evidence of the Crown's expert witness in which he had referred to the Home Office Research Establishment's statistics was admissible.

Reliance on Other Material

In *English Exporters v. Eldonwall Ltd* [1973] 1 Ch 415 Megarry J said that "the opinion of the expert witness is none the worse because it is in part derived from matters of which he could give no direct evidence."

The tenant had applied under the Landlord and Tenant Act 1954 for the grant by the landlords of a new tenancy. The landlords had applied under s.24A of the Act for the determination of an interim rent while the tenancy continued under the provisions of the Act. The Master made an order for one expert on each side. Both were Fellows of the Royal Institution of Chartered Surveyors. There was a considerable measure of agreement between their views. A number of comparables were adduced. Eight were put forward by the landlords; the tenants put in none of their own. It was held by Megarry J that a valuer giving expert evidence:

(a)   may express the opinions he had formed as to values, even though substantial contributions to the formation of these opinions have been made by matters of which he had no first-hand knowledge;

(b)   may give evidence as to details within his personal knowledge, in order to establish them as matters of fact;

(c)   may express his opinion as to the significance of any transactions which are or will be proved to be admissible evidence (whether or not given by him) in relation to the valuation with which he is concerned, but may not give hearsay evidence stating the details of any transactions not within his personal knowledge in order to establish them as matters of fact.

Megarry J explained ... "It makes it no better when the witness expresses his confidence in the reliability of his source of information ... It seems to me that details of comparable transactions upon which the valuer intends to rely in his evidence must, if they are to be put before the court, be confined to those details which have been, or will be proved by admissible evidence, given either by the valuer himself or in some other way. I know of no special rule giving the expert valuation witnesses the right to give hearsay evidence of facts."

The Doctor's Dilemma

A doctor who is called as an expert witness simply to give his opinion does not differ, in the eyes of the law, from any other expert witness. However, it may be that when the doctor is also called as a witness as to fact he may feel that his Hippocratic oath precludes his giving evidence concerning the intimate communications which his patient may have made to him. These communications are not protected in the same way as a client's communications with his legal advisers.

Should a doctor called to give evidence refuse to testify as to what he has learned during a professional consultation, he may be held in contempt of court and sent to prison (*Nuttall v. Nuttall and Twyman* [1964] 108 SJ 605).

However a court may exercise its discretion and allow a doctor to refrain from answering particularly embarrassing and confidential questions. In *Attorney-General v. Mullholland: Attorney-General v. Foster* [1963] 2 QB 477 Lord Denning MR said:

"The only profession that I know which is given a privilege from disclosing information to a court of law is the legal profession and then it is not the privilege of the lawyer but of his client. Take the clergyman, the banker and the medical man. None of these is entitled to refuse to answer when directed by a Judge. Let me not be mistaken. The Judge will respect the confidences which each of these honourable professions receives in the course of it, and will not direct him to answer unless not only is it relevant but also it is a proper and, indeed, necessary question in the course of justice to be put and answered. The Judge is the person entrusted on behalf of the community to weigh these conflicting interests, to weigh on the one hand the respect due to confidence in the profession and on the other hand the ultimate interest of the community in justice being done, e.g. in the case of a tribunal such as this, in a proper investigation being made into these serious allegations."

When a doctor has a witness summons served upon him, requiring his attendance at a trial and requiring him to produce medical reports in his possession relating to a patient, he should not disclose the medical reports to legal advisers for any party in the proceedings until the Judge has ruled whether or not the documents are admissible. In *R. v. Westcott* [1983] Crim LR 545 W was charged with rape, and a witness summons was served on the complainant's general practitioner requiring his attendance at the trial and further requiring him "to produce medical reports in your possession relating to the complainant". The doctor duly attended in compliance with the summons, but handed the records to W's solicitors. The trial Judge refused an application by defending counsel to be allowed to cross-examine the complainant on her medical history. After the jury had retired the Judge indicated to both prosecuting and defending counsel that only in exceptional cases should a summons be issued for a witness to produce medical records relating to the complainant and only when it was shown that there were substantial grounds for thinking that such records contained relevant matters. Where such a summons was issued it should be absolutely clear to the witness that he was only to produce the documents to the court, and not to disclose them to the legal advisers for the prosecution or the defence, until the court has decided whether they should be disclosed.

CHAPTER 8

Hearsay Evidence

"Actual evidence I have none
But my aunt's charwoman's sister's son
Heard a policeman on his beat
Say to a housemaid in Downing Street
That he had a brother, who had a friend
Who knew when the war was going to end."
Reginald Arkell: *All the Rumours, 1916*

Civil Proceedings

Hearsay is defined in the Civil Evidence Act 1995 s.1(2)(a) as a "statement made otherwise than by a person while giving oral evidence in the proceedings which is tendered as evidence of the matter stated." Such proceedings include all civil proceedings and tribunals which are subject to formal rules of evidence.

According to Lord Normand (*Teper v. Regina* (1952) AC 480) hearsay "is not the best evidence and it is not delivered upon oath. The truthfulness and the accuracy of a person whose words are spoken to another witness cannot be tested by cross-examination, and the light which his demeanour would throw on his testimony is lost". However, the Civil Evidence Act 1995, which considerably simplified the law, states that evidence shall not be excluded on the ground that it is hearsay. References to hearsay include hearsay of any degree, ie, it may be first-hand when a witness says what he heard someone else say, or second-hand (or even more distant) when he relates what he was told that someone else said. Hearsay, whether first or second-hand may be oral or documentary, of fact or opinion.

Under s.2(1) of the Act a party proposing to adduce hearsay evidence in civil proceedings must give notice of that fact to the other party and on request provide such particulars as is reasonable and practicable in the circumstances for the purpose of enabling him to deal with any matters arising from it being hearsay.

Weighing the Evidence
The weight which should be attached to hearsay evidence is a matter for the Judge. By s.4 in estimating the weight the court must have regard to any circumstances from which any inferences can reasonably be drawn as to the reliability or otherwise of the evidence. In particular regard may be had to the following:

(a) whether it would have been reasonable and practical for the party by whom the evidence was adduced to have produced the maker of the original statement as a witness;

(b) whether the original statement was made contemporaneously with the occurrence or existence of the matters stated;

(c) whether the evidence involves multiple hearsay;

(d) whether any person involved had any motive to conceal or misrepresent matters;

(e) whether the original statement was an edited account,

or was made in collaboration with another for a particular purpose;

(f)   whether the circumstances in which the evidence is adduced as hearsay are such as to suggest an attempt to prevent proper evaluation of its weight.

Power to Call Witness for Cross-examination on Hearsay Evidence

Where there is a dispute between the parties, the courts have never underestimated the importance of having witnesses present, giving evidence on oath and being subject to cross-examination. By s.3, rules of court provide that where a party to civil proceedings adduces hearsay evidence of a statement made by a person and does not call that person as a witness, any other party to the proceedings may, with the leave of the court, call that person as a witness and cross-examine him on the statement as if he had been called by the first-mentioned party and as if the hearsay statement were his evidence-in-chief. This is an important safeguard against a situation where one party does not wish to put a weak witness into the witness-box where he would be subject to the rigours of cross-examination.

Competence and Credibility

Hearsay evidence will not be admitted in civil proceedings if made by a person suffering from such mental or physical infirmity or lack of understanding as would render a person incompetent as a witness (s.5(1)).

When the maker of an original statement is not called as a witness:

(a) evidence which if he had been so called would be admissible for the purpose of attacking or supporting his credibility as a witness would be admissible for that purpose in the proceedings; and

(b) evidence tending to prove that, whether before or after he made the statement, he made any other statement inconsistent with it, is admissible for the purpose of showing that he had contradicted himself.

Prior to the passing of the Civil Evidence Act 1995 the Law Commission published "The Hearsay Rule in Civil Proceedings (Consultation Paper 177, 1991)" pointing out that the previous rule excluding hearsay was the most confusing of the rules of evidence, posing difficulties for the court, practitioners and witnesses alike. With the advent of the Civil Evidence Act 1995 which received the Royal Assent in November 1995 and came into force on January 31, 1997 this is no longer the case. Confusion should disappear!

Hearsay in Children's Cases

1. *Wardship.* When dealing with wardship cases, the Family Division of the High Court has never considered itself bound by the usual rules of evidence. In *Re K (Infants)* (1965) AC 201 it was held that the court may hear hearsay evidence, ie, what the child or any other person has said. A dispute had arisen over the custody of two children. The Official Solicitor, acting as their guardian *ad litem*, submitted a report to the court in which he set out the contents of interviews he had held with the parents, the children, a doctor and others involved with the children's welfare. The House of Lords held that this hearsay evidence

was properly admitted, in the best interests of the children. Lord Devlin said that the wardship jurisdiction of the court was "more ancient than the rule against hearsay" and he saw no reason why that rule should now be introduced into wardship.

Re K (*Infants*) was followed by the Court of Appeal in *Re W* (*Minors*) (*Wardship: Evidence*) (1990) FCR 286 where it was held that the wardship jurisdiction was a special jurisdiction. The court was put to act on behalf of the Crown, as being the guardian of all minors, in the place of the parent and as if it were the parent of the child, thus superseding the natural guardianship of the child. It was an ancient jurisdiction which had been invoked for centuries. Neill LJ said: "The correct approach to the matter is to recognize that in wardship proceedings, which are of a special kind... hearsay evidence is admissible as a matter of law, but that this evidence and the use to which it is put has to be handled with the greatest care and in such a way that, unless the interests of the child make it necessary, the rules of natural justice and the rights of the parents are fully and properly observed."

2. *Other cases involving the welfare of children.* Where the welfare of the children is the paramount consideration, the courts need to consider not just the facts in issue, but also the future, ie, what is likely to happen, where do the child's best interests lie, what are the wishes and feelings of the children concerned? This task by courts exercising family jurisdiction necessarily expands the scope of the court's investigation. Although the proceedings may well be fiercely contested, there is a growing appreciation that it is inappropriate to regard the issue of the child's welfare as one to be decided solely on the cases presented by the opposing parties. The court has its own investigative and pro-active role.

Rules made under the Children Act 1989 extended the power of courts to allow hearsay evidence. SI 1993 621 states that "In civil proceedings before the High Court or a county court evidence given in connexion with the upbringing, maintenance or welfare of a child shall be admissible notwithstanding any rule of law relating to hearsay" These rules are specifically preserved under the Civil Evidence Act 1995.

Furthermore, in family proceedings, rules prohibiting the admittance of hearsay no longer apply in relation to:

(a)   statements made by children;
(b)   a statement made in any guardian *ad litem* and social inquiry reports; and
(c)   a statement made by a person concerned with or having control of a child, that he has assaulted.

The reason for SI 621 is to ensure that the position of the High Court and the county courts is made absolutely clear when exercising their jurisdiction in children cases, and also to enlarge the powers of the magistrates' courts when they are dealing with children cases.

3. *Inherent danger of hearsay evidence.* The need to exercise great caution in accepting serious allegations, eg, of child sexual abuse, which are not made on oath and therefore are not subject of cross-examination, has greatly troubled the courts.

In *Re K(Infants)* Lord Devlin, after stating that it had always been the practice to admit hearsay in wardship, went on to say: "I cannot imagine that any Judge would allow a grave allegation against a parent to be proved solely by hearsay, at any rate in a case in which direct evidence could be produced."

Neill LJ returned to the same issue in *Re W (Wardship: Evidence)* and quoted from Lord Devlin, above, adding "... it is of crucial important to take account of the saying Lord Devlin himself introduced, namely that a grave allegation against a parent would not be allowed to be proved solely by hearsay `at any rate in a case in which direct evidence could be produced.'"

The matter arose again in *Re P (Child: Compellability as Witness)* [1991] FCR 337, this time in care proceedings. The appellant's step-daughter, aged 17, made allegations of sexual abuse against him. The allegations were strenuously denied by the stepfather and he made efforts to require the girl to give evidence in order that she could be cross-examined and shown to be a liar. The local authority, who instigated the care proceedings, decided not to call the girl. It was common ground that the girl was a compellable witness and was unwilling to give evidence. The Court of Appeal held that an application for judicial review of the local authority's decision not to call the girl could not succeed unless they were acting unreasonably, which was not proved in this case. Butler-Sloss LJ said that a court presented with hearsay evidence has to look at it anxiously and consider carefully the extent to which it can be properly relied upon and went on to cite *Re W (Minors) (Wardship: Evidence)*, which now applies to care proceedings as well as wardship, and quoted Neill LJ's words:

"... hearsay evidence is admissible as a matter of law, but this evidence and the use to which it is put has to be handled with the greatest care and in such a way that, unless the interests of the child make it necessary, the rules of natural justice and the rights of the parents are fully and properly observed."

Criminal Proceedings

Criminal proceedings form a very different background to civil litigation, and there is no statute comparable to the Civil Evidence Act 1995. However, experts have been permitted to give their opinion based on an assumed state of facts. In *R. v. Mason* (1911) 7 Cr App R 67 where the defence to a charge of murder was that the deceased had committed suicide, a doctor who heard the evidence was asked whether it was his opinion that the fatal wound had been inflicted by someone other than the accused. Lord Alverstone CJ said:

> "The question raised is whether the evidence of an expert is admissible when he has not seen the body but has only heard the evidence of those who have. (The doctor had examined the body of the deceased and made careful notes as to the position of the body, the nature of the wounds etc., with a view to forming an opinion as to whether death was caused by suicide or homicide, which was the only issue in the case.) The evidence was clearly admissible and was rightly dealt with in the summing up as an opinion based on an assumed state of facts."

In *R. v. Holmes* (1953) 2 All ER 324 in a trial of the appellant on a charge of murder, the defence raised was that of insanity. The medical witnesses called for both the prosecution and the defence agreed that, at any rate at the time of trial and probably previously, the appellant was suffering from a disease of the mind, a particular form of paranoia. A doctor called for the defence was asked in cross-examination whether the accused's conduct immediately after the incident would indicate that he knew the nature of the act he was committing. Answer: "Yes". The doctor was further asked whether the accused immediately afterwards would indicate that he knew his conduct was contrary to the law of the land. Answer: "Yes". It was contended, on appeal, that the questions were inadmissible on the ground that they were tantamount to asking the doctor to express an opinion on the very issue which the jury had to decide. Held: the questions were rightly admitted.

Latitude allowed in doctor's evidence

Sometimes doctors are asked to give their opinion upon the symptoms which their patients relate to them as having occurred. The case of *R. v. Bradshaw* (1986) 82 Cr App R 79 then applies. Lord Lane CJ said that although as a concession to the defence, where a defendant raises the defence of diminished responsibility to a charge of murder, doctors are sometimes allowed to base their opinions on what the defendant had told them (ie, hearsay) without those matters being proved by admissible evidence; yet a doctor may not state what a parent told him about past symptoms as evidence of those symptoms because that would infringe the law against hearsay. He may, however, give evidence of what the patient told him in order to explain the grounds on which he came to a conclusion with regard to the patient's condition. Lord Lane then made reference to *R. v. Ahmed Din* (1962) 46 Cr App 269, a case of diminished responsibility. These are largely matters of medical opinion, nevertheless where there is any issue on the matter it is for the defence to lay a foundation upon which the experts can give their opinion.

CHAPTER 9

The Expert in the Witness Box

"Let us affirm what seems to be the truth."
Plato: The Dialogues

As the principal aim of this book is to provide help and support to those facing an appearance as an expert witness for the first time, we feel it appropriate to discuss in some detail the expert's position in relation to examination-in-chief and re-examination - ie, by counsel for the party that instructs you - and cross-examination by counsel for the other side.

(a) Examination-in-Chief
The expert witness should always be clear in his own mind, when he enters the witness box, as to the manner in which his counsel is going to take him through his evidence. In these days of increasing pressures pre-trial conferences with counsel are not always as thorough as they used to be, but the expert must establish the *modus operandi* at that time, particularly if he is a novice. It can be damaging to the client's case if the examination-in-chief seems to be more like cross-examination. Counsel should ask short questions but which enable the expert witness to give a full explanation or opinion. The witness will have with him his report (as well as appropriate files, plans and drawings and any other exhibits). On occasion, the

evidence-in-chief will consist solely of the report, copies of which will have been disclosed in advance.

At the outset, counsel will establish the expert witness's name, address, professional qualifications and experience relating to the matter at issue: at this point the expert witness will, normally, be merely be replying in the affirmative. One of the co-authors finds it helpful in keeping fully alert at this stage instead of constantly repeating the answer "yes" to every question, by varying the response, for example to "that is correct", "this is so" etc.

Thereafter, counsel will endeavour to bring out as effectively as possible the main points in the expert witness's report, but he is not permitted to ask leading questions. Some experienced witnesses prefer their counsel to ask general questions, so that they can develop their own statements, but this could be dangerous for the beginner. A common mistake - particularly with inexperienced witnesses - is to repeat the same point, although competent counsel should not allow this to happen.

A common cause for concern is the recognition of a weak point in the expert's case. The authors feel strongly that the best - possibly the only - way of dealing with this is to draw counsel's attention to it at the pre-trial conference and arrange that it is "aired" in full at an early stage. The expert witness can then give in full any mitigating factors or alternative explanation. If the witness gambles on the other side not spotting the weakness and it comes to light in cross-examination, the damage will almost certainly be greater; moreover with the recommended method, the witness's probity and credibility will have been demonstrated early on.

(b) Cross-examination

The authors feel that the most helpful approach is to focus on the significant aspects particular to expert witnesses coupled with a short working list of what they consider are the basic elements of technique required on the part of a witness in dealing with cross-examination.

Whilst expert witnesses are subject to the same basic rules as lay witnesses, the essential difference - the all-important difference - is that an expert, as a result of his training and experience, may include in his evidence opinions he has formed with conclusions he has reached. The opinion of a lay witness based on what he has seen and heard is not admissible. In one of the earliest cases as a young professional man, one of the co-authors was faced with the daunting prospect of cross-examination by distinguished counsel - a QC - and author of a standard textbook on the subject. One question elicited the reply: "That is my opinion." The identical question was repeated and the same response was made - no less than four consecutive times. At this point, the Judge, His Honour Judge Cohen, leant forward and spoke gently to counsel: "I think you will have to accept that that is Mr Smith's opinion." This is the strength of the expert witness's position, but at the same time, puts a special obligation on him.

(c) Re-examination

In re-examination, counsel can only deal with issues that have arisen in cross-examination. If the evidence has been shaken counsel will then strive to make good the damage so far as possible; if the witness has been ambiguous or obtuse, it is up to counsel to simplify the position by skilful questioning.

Demeanour in Court

"Style is the dress of thoughts."

The Earl of Chesterfield 1694-1773
(a letter to a friend concerning poetry)

Speech
The big problem is akin to the golf swing: however many times you practise on your own, all those points of technique evaporate at the moment of performance when you step out to perform in reality. To counter this, the authors suggest that you try and hold tight to just two golden rules:

1. Speak slowly and distinctly. This may sound ridiculously obvious, but in practice, for some people at least, it is extremely difficult to maintain both throughout the hearing. Practise using a dictating machine or cassette player can be of help, particularly if you can get a critical (but patient) friend to provide a question-and-answer scenario for you. Do not try to use words or phrases that are not natural to you: practise the timing of your pauses just as much as the flow of words and the rhythm of your speech.
2. The "Wimbledon" rule. As at a tennis match when your head swivels from side to side as the rally continues, so face counsel when he is addressing you and then turn your head and reply to the tribunal. Watch the same technique being used by a competent public speaker when addressing a large audience.

Do not be despondent after the first time if you feel you have not done justice to the manner in which you have expressed your opinions.

Dress

It does not detract from the value of the expert's evidence if he appears in clothes more suitable for leisure activities. However, we believe that the expert will feel more in tune with the atmosphere of a formal hearing when wearing neat, relatively sober and well-styled clothes. One of the co-authors vividly recalls the appearance of the late Sir Keith Simpson, the distinguished pathologist, when giving evidence to the Crown Court at Croydon some years ago. He was impeccably dressed in a well-cut navy suit which hung from beautifully padded shoulders, with an immaculate white shirt and sporting a discreet tie. His hair was neatly cut and well brushed. Sir Keith stood in the witness box with an unchallengeable air of confidence, exuding infinite expertise. What was the case about? That particular fact completely escapes our recollection.

Another aspect of the importance of dressing appropriately is revealed by the following story told to the authors by a former distinguished Judge. As a young barrister he appeared in a case in which a dental surgeon was giving evidence as an expert witness before that most formidable of Judges, Lord Goddard. Somewhat against the odds, they won the case. Over a celebratory drink the barrister, noting that the dental surgeon was sporting the old boy's tie of a famous public school (where the barrister himself had been a pupil) commented:

"I didn't know you were an Old M..."
E.W.: "I'm not."
"Then why are you wearing the tie?"
E.W.: "Last night I looked up Lord Goddard in 'Who's Who' and found out that he had been to school there."

The authors wish to make it absolutely clear that they do not recommend this tactic and disclaim any responsibility for the anecdote.

Ten Golden Rules

1. Speak clearly: if you can best achieve this by speaking slowly, do so - but not painfully slowly.
2. Listen carefully to the questions: allow yourself time to think, and if you do not fully understand the question, politely ask for it to be repeated.
3. Answer only what is asked.
4. Be as brief as possible, consistent with answering the question.
5. Use simple words, and avoid jargon or technical terms.
6. Acknowledge your professional limitations, if a question is beyond your competence.
7. Do not evade a question: if you do not know, say so clearly and unambiguously.
8. Answer calmly: do not argue.
9. If you do not agree, disagree firmly and repeatedly but without heat.
10. If you make a mistake, say so and apologize. If you made the mistake earlier, be brave enough to point this out - however late in the day.

CHAPTER 10

The Expert Witness as Advocate

> "'Advocacy' the highest gift of providence to man,
> needs the assistance of many arts ..."
>
> Quintilian (42-118 AD)

General Principles

There may be occasions when the expert witness will also be required to act as advocate. This is not permissible in the Divisional Court, county courts or magistrates' courts - indeed in any court-of-law - where advocacy is restricted to barristers and solicitors, apart from persons who choose to act on their own behalf. The Lands Tribunal does have a discretion in this regard, but has rarely permitted anyone other than lawyers to appear as advocates in the professional sense. However, this is perfectly permissible before such quasi-judicial bodies as rent assessment committees, valuation and community charge tribunals and rent tribunals - and also before arbitrators and town planning inspectors.

Of course, the expert must be reasonably satisfied that he will be able to perform the task of advocacy with some degree of competency; further, he would probably be unwise to make the attempt if there are any points of law involved, or if the issues are particularly complicated. If he does decide to proceed, then the problem is - how to successfully combine the contrasting dual roles?

One of the co-authors confesses to a certain cynicism here: at the start of his career he found the prospect worrying and was uncertain how he could clearly demonstrate the switch in the course of the proceedings. However, in practice, he soon discovered that the tribunal concerned was either unaware of the distinction, or apparently chose to ignore it.

Be that as it may, this is begging the question. It is the responsibility of the expert to inform - and if necessary describe - his dual role to the tribunal. The simplest method of doing this is for the expert to explain at the outset what his instructions are and how he proposes to deal with these at the various stages of the proceedings, emphasizing the changeover points in particular. The layout of the hearing room can be of positive help, particularly if a witness stand is provided. After the expert has made his initial statement as advocate, he can move over to the stand to give his examination-in-chief as expert witness and subsequently, if necessary, carry out re-examination of himself. Thereafter, he can resume his original place and concurrently his role as advocate.

It is essential for the expert to fully appreciate the demarcation lines between the expert witness and the advocate before attempting both roles. In general terms both have a duty to the tribunal, but thereafter their paths diverge. In addition to this duty - which patently is of paramount importance - the advocate has his responsibilities to his client. His job is to put the case on behalf of his client, to convince the tribunal that he is right and that the other side is wrong. He has a duty to cite all appropriate statutory provisions and all relevant cases. As to matters of fact he may - quite properly - emphasize only those which aid his client's cause and disregard those that do not.

Finally, in subsequent similar cases, the advocate may change his submissions on behalf of another client.

By contrast, the function of the expert witness is to assist the tribunal in arriving at their judgment by providing facts and opinions on technical matters. He does not make any submissions: he expresses his personal conclusions. He must put forward all relevant facts known to him whether these are helpful - or positively unhelpful - to his client's case. In fact, it is at this point that there is the greatest likelihood that the dual role play may come into conflict. In the case of *Multi-media Productions Ltd v. Secretary of State for the Environment* [1988] 5 CLD 0318, which concerned an appeal against a refusal of planning permission, it was held that whilst there is no rule against a person combining the roles of expert witness and advocate before a public local inquiry, it was an undesirable practice. An expert witness had to give a true and unbiased opinion; the advocate had to do his best for his client. The expert who had also played the role of advocate should not be surprised if his evidence was later treated by a court with some caution.

It should be noted that these remarks made by Mr David Widdicombe QC (sitting as a Deputy High Court Judge) were in the context of a public local inquiry, where the Planning Officer combined both roles on behalf of his full-time employers. In the opinion of the co-authors, these strictures need not apply before tribunals where the expert is not on the payroll of the parties and is self-employed.

Advocacy

One of the greatest advocates of the twentieth century, the late Lord Birkett, once wrote that the first and vital thing (*sic*) is that the advocate shall know the case that he desires to make with complete thoroughness. Whilst the "amateur" advocate cannot hope to match the skills of a Norman Birkett, he should always aspire to follow this directive. The second point to remember is one given to the non-legal co-author at the start of his career by his then senior partner: "It's not given to all of us to be fluent, but anybody can be brief." Brevity is particularly important in your opening statement. Counsel may, on occasion, go into a certain amount of detail of what his witness is going to say: this is patently superfluous in the dual role situation as immediately after the opening, the expert will revert to being a witness and give his evidence-in-chief. (Technically speaking, you will under one hat be cross-examining yourself under the other.)

A book of this nature is not the place to discuss the finer points of advocacy. However, we offer a working rule which we hope will combat the principal errors: the two main types of approach from beginners: on the one hand, taciturn reticence (the "let's get it over and done with as fast as possible" school) and the other prolix verbosity ("the rush of blood to the head" school). A middle course can be steered by remembering at all times to distinguish between law, facts and opinions; between relevant facts and irrelevant facts; between agreed facts and the facts in issue.

Cross-examination is an art of its own - as you may soon learn for yourself when on the receiving end of questioning by able counsel! Sometimes the most astute judgment may lie in deciding not to make any cross-examination at all. If you opt to proceed, bear in mind at all times that the purpose is not only negative, i.e. to weaken the case for the other side, but also positive in that you are trying to establish facts favourable to your case.

The temptation for the amateur advocate in a situation where he knows he can establish facts differing from the evidence given by the witness for the other side is to rush in and demolish the opposition in the TV drama style. But first the cross-examiner must get the witness to commit himself unreservedly to the viewpoint of the cross-examiner. The other major temptation for the novice is to go on for too long, particularly of course when he is having a measure of success, but this is where real judgmental skill is required. The point was well illustrated by the late Richard Du Cann, QC in *The Art of the Advocate* (an excellent book which the co-authors unhesitatingly recommend for those who wish to know more of this whole subject).

"A young man was once charged with having unlawful sexual intercourse with a girl under sixteen. The corroborative evidence supporting the girl's story came from a farmer who said he had seen a pair lying together in a field.
   He was asked:

Counsel: When you were a young man, did you never take a girl for a walk in the evening?
Farmer: Aye, that I did.
Counsel: Did you ever sit and cuddle her on the grass in a field?
Farmer: Aye, that I did.
Counsel: And did you never lean over and kiss her while she was lying back?
Farmer: Aye, that I did.
Counsel: Anybody in the next field, seeing that, might easily have thought you were having sexual intercourse with her?

Farmer: Aye, and they'd have been right too."

The point made by Mr Du Cann is that the last question should always be to the disadvantage of the witness: in the above example, the cross-examiner could not resist the temptation to go on and his last question destroyed all the previous effect.

The authors hope that the following skeleton plan of campaign may assist the novice to cross-examine effectively.

1. Prepare your material thoroughly before launching into cross-examination. On occasions there may be relatively little time available between concluding your evidence, taking notes of the evidence from the other side and stepping up as advocate, in which event it may be wiser to limit your cross-examination to one or two questions on the most crucial issues.

2. Set down a plan of your cross-examination, possibly in tabular form, but in any event in a format that will enable you to deal with the witness most effectively. Some people operate better by working only from headings, others by writing down every relevant question that they intend to ask. This is a matter of personal taste for the beginner to resolve.

3. Keep the cross-examination concise, controlled and clear, so that the witness is not given a chance to put forward material detrimental to your case.

4. Be on the alert to establish a particular point of view, or particular matter of fact, at the most telling moment. It is counter-productive to enter into a series of basic questions, which may very well enable the witness to introduce a new matter that is unhelpful, or to reiterate the strong points already made in his evidence.

5. Try to remain courteous to witnesses even if - perhaps particularly if - they are being rude and offensive to you. The authors firmly believe the rapier is more effective than the bludgeon. Moreover, offensive language and demeanour may well lead the tribunal to interrupt, which they will not be disposed to do if the cross-examiner remains courteous and is putting forward questions that are relevant. The tribunal will be inclined to give greater assistance to "amateur" counsel who are conducting their cross-examination properly than to a witness who is unresponsive and unhelpful.

In making your closing submissions, we recommend that you summarize your case by breaking this down into the main points you wish to emphasize, reiterating each of these in a concise fashion to the tribunal, clearly distinguishing each one. This should be done slowly enough to permit the members to write down the essence of your case. At the same time, clearly distinguish each point from the others: the tribunal are no doubt writing as fast as they can and it is easy for the members to become confused if you are putting your case in a jumbled, illogical fashion. Further, the weak points in your opponent's case can be commented upon, and it is perfectly proper in addition to draw your own conclusions on these, but only where their witnesses have been cross-examined by you on those points: no new issues can be raised at this final stage.

Then all you can do is to await the decision of the tribunal (and decide whether or not to appeal!).

Duties

The duties of advocate and expert witness contrasted.

Advocate
Paramount Duty: To the court towards a correct and just decision.

1. By means of submitting a case for his client.

2. Must cite all relevant cases and statutory provisions.
3. Concurrently has a duty to his client to present his case to try to convince the court that he is right and that the other side is wrong.
4. In so doing may omit facts at his discretion, if this be of advantage to his client.
5. May change submissions on behalf of client in subsequent similar cases.

Expert Witness
Paramount Duty: To the court towards a correct and just decision.

1. By means of informing the court of his opinion, and assisting with facts and technical matters.
2. Has no duty to cite cases or statutes.
3. Expert witness speaks for himself and does not make submissions.
4. Must put forward all relevant facts.
5. The expert's opinion should remain constant (in the absence of any new material to the contrary).

CHAPTER 11

Expert Witnesses in Arbitration Cases

"And that old common arbitrator, Time, will one day end it."
Shakespeare, Troilus and Cressida. IV

Arbitration is one possible method of dispute resolution. Other methods include litigation, negotiation, mediation, adjudication, and expert determination.

Adjudication is a quick and temporary process by which a third party reaches a decision which remains binding until the contract is completed and the dispute is finalized, eg, the Housing Grants, Construction and Regeneration Act 1996, s.108 gives a party to a construction contract the right to refer a dispute arising out of the contract for adjudication. The decision of the adjudicator, who has a duty to act impartially, remains binding until the dispute is finally determined by legal proceedings, by arbitration or by agreement.

Expert Determination is often confused with arbitration. In both, the dispute is resolved by the decision of a third person appointed by the agreement of the parties. In arbitration, the parties further agree to a procedure whereby evidence, including that of expert witnesses if need be, and argument are put forward to the arbitrator who may himself be an expert. His decision is based on the evidence and the argument which he has heard. In expert determination, an expert in the field is appointed to determine the issue on the basis of his own expertise. The expert is the tribunal, not an expert witness. The process is informal and so long as the basic rules of natural justice are observed, the process cannot be successfully challenged. The expert determination has considerable freedom, eg, there is no need for a hearing; the decision can be made without the parties being aware of the results of any investigation. The process is most frequently used in rent review disputes, where the parties agree to have their differences resolved by an expert valuer. The determination cannot be enforced as an arbitral award, although it is a final and binding decision.

The differences between arbitration and expert determination are considerable, not only in relation to procedures but also in regard to the legal position of the determinator. The expert witness should be aware of these and accordingly they are summarized in Appendix III.

The Essence of Arbitration

The arbitration reference is held in private. It follows that the discussions of the parties, their business relationship and the actions of the parties will not be revealed to a sometimes curious local or business community. Even the fact that a reference to arbitration has been made will not become public knowledge, unless the parties so wish.

The parties choose their own arbitrator. In doing so they may agree to appoint a lawyer versed in the legal niceties which may arise. Or they may agree that someone familiar with their particular field, eg, a quantity surveyor or an engineer in a construction dispute, would be preferable.

The parties can choose their venue for all or part of the proceedings. A discreet country hotel may find favour, or a pleasant little known remote island! They can also choose the law they wish to be applied. This may be of considerable importance in an international arbitration. They may also choose the language or languages in which the arbitration will be conducted.

After the passing of the Arbitration Act 1996 it was claimed that arbitration would be less expensive and involve less delay than litigation. However, with the coming into force of the Civil Procedure Rules 1998 this is a contention now open to dispute. Arbitration does not of itself hasten any process of resolution - it only makes it possible, if the parties are willing. However by s.33 of the Arbitration Act a general duty is imposed on the arbitral tribunal to act fairly and impartially and to avoid unnecessary delay or expense.

Commencement of the Arbitration

Procedures for starting an arbitration depend upon what the parties have agreed as the first step to be taken. The parties are free to agree when the arbitration is to be regarded as commenced, both for the purposes of the Arbitration Act 1996, and for the purpose of the Limitation Act 1980. If there is no such agreement, arbitral proceedings are begun when one party serves written notice on the other party, requiring him to appoint or agree to the appointment of an arbitrator.

Is the Dispute within the Terms of the Arbitration Act 1996?

The provisions of the Arbitration Act 1996 apply only where the arbitration agreement is in writing (s.5(i)). An "arbitration agreement" is an agreement to submit to arbitration present or future disputes (s.6(i)).

The provisions are founded on the general principles set out in s.1, ie:

(a) The object of arbitration is to obtain the fair resolution of disputes by an impartial tribunal without unnecessary delay or expense.

(b) The parties should be free to agree how their disputes are resolved, subject only to such safeguards as are necessary in the public interest.

(c) In matters governed by the Act, the court should not interfere except as provided by the Act.

The whole thrust of the Act is to give autonomy to the parties, so long as they can agree with one another and their agreement is in writing. The role of the court is to support the arbitral process.

Procedure and Evidential Matters

By s.34(2)(c) of the Arbitration Act 1996, the parties have the right to agree whether any and if so what form of written statement of claim and defence are to be used, when these should be supplied and the extent to which such statements can be later amended.

Other sub-sections of s.34(2) which are of interest to an expert witness are:

(d)   Whether any and if so which documents or classes of documents should be disclosed between and produced by the parties and at what stage.

(e)   Whether any and if so what questions should be put to and answered by the respective parties and when and in what form this should be done.

(f)   Whether to apply strict rules of evidence (or any other rules) as to the admissibility, relevance, or weight of any material (oral, written or other) sought to be tendered on any matters of fact or opinion, and the time, manner and form in which such material should be exchanged.

Thus, the parties have the right to choose any form of procedural and evidential matters. It is of vital importance that the expert witnesses as well as the arbitrators should be informed of the agreements.

Where no Arbitration Agreement Exists

If there is no arbitration agreement already in existence the parties may, for the same reasons which apply in drawing up a prior arbitration agreement, find it preferable to make a submission to arbitration rather than resort to litigation. By doing so, they can keep some control and guard some privacy over their own affairs, rather than having them revealed in the fair but public arena of the courts, for their friends and rivals to gossip and wonder upon.

The same point applies, ie, the expert and the arbitrator should be informed of the rules of procedure which has been agreed upon between the parties.

Power of the Arbitration Tribunal to Appoint Experts

Unless otherwise agreed by the parties the tribunal can:

(i)   appoint experts or legal advisers to report to it and the parties, or

(ii)   appoint assessors to assist it on technical matters, and may allow any such expert, legal adviser or assessor to attend the proceedings (Arbitration Act 1996 Sec.37(I)).

This power of the tribunal to itself appoint experts goes further than that of a Judge in litigation (see Chapter 3).

The parties must have a reasonable opportunity to correct any information, opinion or advice proffered by any expert, legal adviser or assessor. The arbitrators are liable for their fees and, as expenses, can therefore form part of the tribunal's award on costs.

Conduct of Proceedings

It is likely that the procedure will be much more flexible than litigation in the High Court. However by agreement between the parties or by direction of the tribunal there will probably be provision for prior exchange of expert witnesses' reports, and for examination and cross-examination upon the report at the hearing if "written reports only" has not been agreed. Therefore, the same degree of preparation and care which we have counselled in relation to court proceedings also apply in arbitration proceedings.

The expert witnesses can expect that the procedure adopted will allow for each party to present their case fully, and the opening to the arbitral tribunal will include reference to the facts as well as the law, whether or not the arbitrator is a lawyer. Each party will be given full opportunity to examine and test the case of the other side. An arbitral decision can be made, by agreement between the parties, without any oral hearing taking place. In that case the reports of the expert witnesses will be sent to the arbitrator together with submissions and statements of other witnesses. If the expert is called at any oral hearing to give evidence he will, of course, have prior sight of the report of the expert called by the other side. It would be sensible to find out whether the arbitrator will be a lawyer or someone who is an expert in this particular specialized field which the expert witness is covering.

In general, the expert witness may expect the position to be as in *Chiltern v. Saga Holidays PLC* (1986) 1 All ER 841 where reference as made to Russell on the Law of Arbitration which quotes Lord Cranworth LC in *Drew v. Drew* (1855) 2 Macq 1: "The principles of universal justice require that the person who is to be prejudiced by evidence ought to be present to hear it taken, to suggest cross-examination or himself cross-examine, and to be able to find, if he can, that which shall meet and answer it, as in the ordinary course of legal proceedings."

The role of the expert, whomsoever calls him as a witness, is to assist the arbitrator in respect of the technical issues relating to the dispute. His primary duty, as in litigation, is to the tribunal, not the parties.

Flexibility under the Arbitration Act 1996

The Act sets out to give autonomy to the parties. Subject to public interest safeguards they can agree how they will resolve their disputes. The Act was passed against a background of decline in the use of arbitration, particularly in big commercial cases. This could be attributed to the increasing number of lawyers engaged in arbitration practice together with the increase of lawyers appointed as the arbitral tribunal. Furthermore, arbitration had become an increasingly expensive form of dispute resolution. This led to greater reliance on the tried and tested legal procedures of the courts. The justification for their use was that each party, on the advice of legal advisers, wished to take every opportunity to employ all safeguards to ensure his cases was presented fully and fairly to the arbitral tribunal.

So far as the expert is concerned, whether in the compilation of his report or in the giving of evidence in arbitration cases, he must be prepared to conform to the procedure and form of evidence agreed upon by the parties.

The Expert as an Arbitrator

In a number of arbitration agreements there is provision for the appointed arbitrator to himself be an expert; eg, the Institution of Civil Engineers, the Royal Institute of British Architects, and the Royal Institution of Chartered Surveyors maintain lists from which arbitrators are appointed in suitable cases.

The expert witness giving evidence therefore not only has to contend with questions from counsel for the other party, but maybe also from the arbitrator himself, knowledgeable in his own subject.

"There can be no doubt that the arbitrator is entitled to form his own opinion, despite the views offered by the experts. The question is: what the arbitrator should do if he forms a view outside the range of opinions offered by the experts?" (*Fox and Others v. Wellfair* (1981) 2 Lloyds Reports 514). The expert arbitrator was enjoined to remind himself of his judicial role by Dunn LJ: "An expert arbitrator can rely on his general knowledge of comparable rents in the district. But if he knows of a particular comparable case, then he should disclose details of it before relying on it for his award." Dunn LJ went on to say that natural justice required that the arbitrator should have put his alternative scheme and alternative costings to the experts to give them an opportunity of dealing with them.

In *Bremner Vulkan v. S. India Shipping Co.* (1980) 2 WLR 905 Roskill LJ expressed the view that an arbitrator or umpire who, in the absence of express agreement that he should do so, attempts to conduct an arbitration along inquisitorial lines might expose himself to criticism and possible removal.

Thus we see that the expert appointed as an arbitrator must take great care to ensure that each party has the opportunity to present his case, call relevant evidence in support of his argument, test the evidence put forward by the other side and have an opportunity to address the tribunal on the issues between the parties, as well as being present throughout the whole of the hearing.

The expert arbitrator may sometimes feel that if only he could be allowed to give his expert opinion on the issue, the matter could be more easily resolved. That is not his role when sitting as the arbitral tribunal and although no doubt he has been appointed for his own wide experience in the particular specialist field, he must be careful not to substitute his own expertise for that of the experts called by the parties. An arbitrator has the same ultimate duty as a Judge, ie, to choose between two versions of the truth, as presented by the parties. Where the parties employ an arbitrator who has expert knowledge and experience and authorize him to make use of those qualities, it is, of course, proper for him to do so. This frequently happens in the construction industry or a "quality arbitration" on perishable goods.

The arbitrator will of course have to accept the parties' agreed methods of procedure and presentation of evidential matter. Section 34(I) states that it shall be for the tribunal to decide on procedural and evidential matters, subject to the right of the parties to agree any matter. There is no reason, however, why the arbitrator should not assist the parties to reach an agreement at an early stage of the proceedings.

Criticism has been voiced from time to time that some arbitrators have conducted themselves on a too "friendly user" basis. It is very important that both parties feel that they are appearing before a neutral tribunal which does not appear to favour one side more than the other. Arbitrators would be well advised to have their lunch alone and to have separate toilet facilities, if possible. Neither party could then imagine that the arbitrator was finding the other party had more amusing jokes, and therefore a better case. Impartiality, and the appearance of impartiality must be maintained.

CHAPTER 12

Liability of the Expert Witness

"All men are liable to error: and most men are, in many
points, by passion or interest, under temptation to it."
John   Locke   1632-1704,   Essay   Concerning   Human
Understanding

Negligence Defined

Negligence is defined in the Unfair Contract Terms Act 1977
s.1. as the breach:

(a)   of any obligation arising from the expressed or implied
       term of a contract to take reasonable care or exercise
       of a reasonable skill in the performance of the contract;
(b)   of any common law duty to take reasonable care or
       exercise reasonable skill (but not any stricter duty).

Appointment in the Ordinary Course of Professional Business

If an expert is engaged in doing work which requires his
expertise, he has undertaken to bring to the exercise a
reasonable degree of skill and care.

In *Whitehouse v. Jordan* (1981) 1 WLR 246 Lord Fraser referred to the test of what a party is entitled to expect from an expert he employs as "the standard skill expected from the ordinary competent specialist having regard to the experience and expertise that a specialist holds himself out as possessing."

The concept is not new. In *Lanphier v. Phipos* (1838) 8 C and P 475 Tindal CJ said:

> "Every person who enters into a learned profession undertakes to bring to the exercise of it a reasonable degree of skill and care. He does not undertake, if he is an attorney, that at all events you shall gain your case, nor does a surgeon undertake he will perform a cure, nor does he undertake to use the highest possible degree of skill."

Where there is a contract for the supply of services such as an expert would provide, it is normally an implied term of the contract that the supplier will carry out the service with reasonable care and skill. Thus in the case of a contract for the supply of professional services, the supplier must exercise the degree of care and skill which is to be expected of a professional person of ordinary care and experience. If he fails to do so, he will be liable in negligence. In *Bolam v. Friern Hospital Management Committee* (1957) 1 WLR 582 it was held that a doctor who acted in accordance with a practice accepted at the time as proper by a reasonable body of medical opinion skilled in the particular form of treatment was not guilty of negligence merely because there was a body of competent professional opinion which might adopt a different technique. As McNair J said:

"In an ordinary case it is generally said you judge it by the action of the man in the street. He is the ordinary man. In one case it has been said you judge it by the conduct of the man on the top of a Clapham omnibus. He is the ordinary man. But where you get a situation which involved the use of some special skill or competence, then the test as to whether there has been negligence or not is not the test of the man on top of a Clapham omnibus, because he has not got this special skill. The test is the standard of the ordinary skilled man exercising and professing to have that special skill. A man need not possess the highest expert skill; it is well established law that it is sufficient if he exercises the ordinary skill of an ordinary competent man exercising that particular art."

This case was applied in the House of Lords in *In Re F (Mental Patient: Sterilization)* [1989] 2 WLR 1025. Lord Bridge said (at p.1064):

"It follows that if the professionals in question have acted with due skill and care, judged by the well-known test laid down in *Bolam v. Friern Hospital Management Committee* they should be immune from liability in trespass (to the person) just as they are immune in negligence."

Learned writers such as Charlesworth and Percy on "Negligence" (9th edn, Sweet and Maxwell 1997) remind us that it should be borne in mind that the *Bolam* test is of general application and is not confined to a defendant exercising or professing the particular skill of medicine.

If an action for negligence is to succeed, damage must have been suffered by the claimant (*Foster v. Outred and Co.* (1982)

(CA) WLR 86). Therefore the two elements which must be proved by the party alleging negligence at the hands of the expert are:

(a) Negligence must be established according to the definition given above.

(b) Actual damages have been suffered by the client as the result of negligence.

The expert will be covered by professional indemnity insurance for work done in the normal course of his ordinary practice and this will include any advice given professionally in his capacity as an expert. The policy of insurance will thus cover any claims for negligence, alleged or actual. The best, and obvious, advice we can give to the expert is to look carefully at his insurance policy at the same time as providing a thorough and competent report. We would emphasize that the expert is only expected to take proper care, not necessarily to please his clients.

The facts of *Whitehouse v. Jordan* are worth some consideration. Stuart Whitehouse was born with severe brain damage and he claimed, through his mother, as his litigation friend, that the damage to his brain was caused by the professional negligence of Mr Jordan, a senior registrar at the hospital in Birmingham where the birth took place. The negligence ultimately charged against Mr Jordan was that in the course of carrying out a "trial of forceps delivery" he pulled too long and too strongly upon the child's head, thereby causing brain damage. The trial Judge, in a case lasting 11 days, heard eminent medical experts on each side and found that the claimant had proved his case. The Court of Appeal, by a majority, reversed the decision. The House of Lords upheld the Court of Appeal. Lord Wilberforce pointed out that in order to establish liability, or to obtain an award of compensation against a doctor or hospital, the plaintiff had to prove that there had been negligence in law.

Lord Edmund Davies quoted from the judgment of McNair J in *Bolam v. Friern Hospital Management Committee,* thus reiterating that the test is the standard of the ordinary skilled man exercising and professing to have that special skill.

Lord Russell said that not all errors of judgment showed a lapse from the standards of skill and care required to be exercised to avoid a charge of negligence.

A charge of professional negligence is a serious matter. Lord Denning MR in *Hucks v. Cole (The Times,* May 9, 1968) pointed out that it stands on a different footing to a charge of negligence against a driver of a motor car. The consequences are far more. "It affected professional status and reputation. The burden was consequently greater. As the charge was so grave, so should the proof be clear."

Lord Justice Sedley in *Michael Hyde v. L.D. Williams (C A) (The Times,* September 4, 2000) said that where the particular profession itself embraced more than one tenable view or acceptable practice, competence would not be measurable by a single forensically determined standard; so that where there was more than one acceptable standard, competence had to be gauged by the lowest of them.

Testimony of Witnesses

The basic principles were set out a long time ago. In *R. v. Skinner* [1772] Lofft 55 Lord Mansfield said:

"Neither party, witness, counsel, jury or Judge can be put to answer, civilly or criminally, for words spoken in the office. If the words are opprobrious or irrelevant to the case, the court will take notice of them as contempt and examine on information. If anything of *mala mens* evil thoughts is found on such inquiry, it will be punished suitably."

We will first deal with perjury, and then immunity from civil actions.

Perjury

In common with all witnesses, if an expert tells lies on his oath he is liable to a criminal prosecution for perjury, under the Perjury Act 1911. By s.1(1) the prosecution would have to prove:

(a) that the person was lawfully sworn as a witness;
(b) in a judicial proceeding (which includes any court, tribunal or person by law having the power to hear, receive, and examine evidence on oath);
(c) that the witness made the statement wilfully, ie, deliberately, and not by mistake;
(d) that the statement was false;
(e) that the witness knew it was false or did not believe it to be true;
(f) that the statement was material to the judicial proceeding.

It would be for the Judge to decide this matter. We do not know of any case where an expert witness has been prosecuted for perjury.

Absolute Immunity of Witnesses from a Civil Action

The basic reasons for the immunity of witnesses were stated by Lord Salmon in *Sutcliffe v. Thackrah* [1974] AC 727:

"It is well settled that Judges, barristers, solicitors, jurors and witnesses enjoy an absolute immunity from any civil action being brought against them in respect of anything they say or do in court during the course of a trial. This is not because the law regards any of these with special tenderness, but because the law recognizes that, on balance of convenience, public policy demands that they shall all have immunity. It is of great importance that all shall perform their respective functions free from fear that disgruntled and possibly impecunious persons who have lost their case or been convicted may subsequently harass them with litigation ... The law takes the risk of their being negligent and confers upon them the privilege from inquiry in an action as to whether or not they have been so. The immunity which they enjoy is vital to the efficient and speedy administration of justice."

In this case the claimant employed the defendants, a firm of architects, to design a house for him. Subsequently he entered into a contract with a firm of builders to build the house. The contract was in the RIBA standard form. The defendants were appointed architects and quantity surveyors. During the carrying out of the works they issued interim certificates to the builders. Before the builders had completed the work the claimant turned them off the site and another firm completed the work at higher cost. The original builders subsequently went into liquidation.

The claimant brought an action against the defendants for negligence, breach of duty in supervising the building of the house and in certifying for work not done, or improperly done, by the builders. It was held that in issuing interim certificates, an architect did not, apart from specific agreement, act as an arbitrator between the parties, and that he was under a duty to act fairly in making his evaluation, and was liable to an action in negligence at the suit of the building owner.

The case illustrates the differences between an expert acting in the usual course of his professional business, and when giving evidence at trial as an expert witness. In the former capacity he is liable in negligence, in the latter he is not. As Lord Salmon observed. "This appeal raises the immediate question as to whether or not an immunity against being sued for negligence extends to an architect who, because of his negligence, has caused damage to his client. This question cannot, however, be satisfactorily answered without considering a wider issue, namely the limits of immunity which the law affords against claims of negligence in general." Lord Salmon then explained the reasons why immunity is given to witnesses in a trial, as stated above.

In *Marrivan v. Vibrani* 1963 1 QB 528 the Court of Appeal held that in addition to being protected in court proceedings, witnesses were also protected in the collection, analysis and preparation of material relevant to the court appearance.

This was followed in *Palmer v. Durnford* (1992) QB 483. An expert was retained by the plaintiff to advise them as to whether, from an engineering point of view, a civil claim was justified. Prior to the trial there was mutual disclosure of documents. On seeing the other side's reports, the expert advised that he would have difficulty supporting the claim against one of the defendants. At the trial the claimants abandoned their claims after the expert had given evidence. Simon Tuckey QC, sitting as a deputy High Court Judge, held that, in accordance with decided cases, an expert retained for the purpose of litigation is immune from liability for the evidence he gives in court; also for the work done in preparation for this purpose, including preparing a report for the purpose of disclosure to the other side. However, the expert is not immune in respect of advice given to a client as to the merits of the claim.

Advice Only Does Not Attract Immunity

Immunity does not extend to protect an expert who has been retained to advise as to the merits of a party's claim in litigation from a suit by the party by whom he had been retained in respect of that advice. This applies notwithstanding that it was in contemplation at the time when the advice was given that the expert would be a witness at the trial if that litigation were to proceed.

Meeting of Experts Before Trial

In *Stanton v. Callagan* 1998 (4 AER 961) the Court of Appeal held that a new category attracting immunity should be added, ie, on the grounds of public interest. With the agreement of their insurers, the claimants carried out partial underpinning to their house which suffered from subsidence, but the work failed to stabilise the property. Subsequently they engaged the defendant, a civil and structural engineer, to make a report. On the claimant's instructions the defendant attended a meeting at the property with the expert instructed on behalf of the insurers (who had refused to pay out on the claimant's claim against them).

Following the meeting, the defendant and the insurer's expert signed a joint statement and as a consequence the defendant revised his draft report. This did not please the claimants, who alleged that the defendant had acted negligently. The defendant contended that as an expert witness he could not be sued for work he had done in preparation for the trial as he was protected on the principle of witness immunity.

I he Court of Appeal held that an expert who prepared a joint statement in conjunction with the expert instructed by the other party, for the purpose of indicating what matters were or were not in issue between them, was immune from suit by the party who had retained him in respect of that statement. That was so notwithstanding that he did not give evidence in the trial, either because it did not take place or because he was not called as a witness. Such immunity was justified because the public interest in facilitating full and frank discussion before trial requires that each expert should be free to make proper concessions without fear that any departure from advice previously given to the party who retained him would be seen as evidence of negligence. It was also needed in order to avoid the tension between a desire to assist the court and fear of the consequences of a departure from previous advice.

CHAPTER 13

Terms of Appointment

"Wilt thou seal up the avenues of ill?
Pay every debt, as if God wrote the bill."
Ralph Waldo Emerson 1803-1882

Relying on the principles of the law of contract, an expert witness is entitled to look to the party who instructed him for the payment of fees. The agreement on fees and terms of engagement should be clearly set out in writing before the expert commences work (not "your usual fee will be met").

Where a solicitor instructs an expert to provide a report and be available to give testimony in court, the Law Society's Code of Conduct applies, unless there is an agreement to the contrary. The solicitor is personally responsible for paying the proper costs of any professional agent whom he instructs on behalf of his client whether or not he receives payment by his client.

The Law Society's Code of Practice relating to expert witnesses engaged by solicitors set out, *inter alia*:

"Terms of Business"
Experts should provide Terms of Business for agreement with the instructing solicitors. These should include:

(a) daily or hourly rates of the experts to be engaged on the assignment or alternatively an agreed reasonable fee for the project or for the services;
(b) treatment of travelling time;
(c) likely expenses and disbursements;
(d) contingency provision for payment of a specified fee in the event of late notice of cancellation of a court hearing;
(e) provision for preferred timing of payment, including any special provisions where the case is legally aided or the fees are to be paid in a third party.

The expert should be made aware, and have confirmed in his terms of appointment, whether he is required to provide a written report only or whether in addition he will be required to attend hearings and appointments or meetings arranged with other experts (other than those ordered by the court). The helpful "Model Terms of Engagement" issued by the Academy of Experts deal in some further detail with these matters.

After a case has been concluded the solicitor is entitled to go before the Taxing Master of the court, to justify his bill of costs, including the fee for the expert witness. An expert has no *locus standi* in his own right before a Taxing Master although the solicitor is entitled to bring him along to justify the fee.

Contingency Fees

Some litigants, particularly in the commercial field, would like to extend the scheme of "no win, no fee" litigation to the payment of fees of experts whose services have been provided. This is not advisable. In their "Model Terms of Engagement" (January 2000) the Academy of Experts is quite specific:

> "The instruction and remuneration of the Expert is not made on any contingent or conditional basis and any payment sought to be made on such a basis will not be acceptable."

The need for an expert's duty of independence and impartiality is inconsistent with the receiving of a contingency fee (which means that an expert witness has a direct financial interest in the outcome of the case). Such a direct financial interest increase the pressures on expert witnesses to give evidence that favours their client. Even if an expert witness resists this pressure, his independence may still be compromised. An expert witness must not only be independent, he must be seen to be independent.

Professional Indemnity

An expert acting as an adviser will be covered for work done in this capacity by the insurance policy taken out to cover the normal practice of his primary profession (see Chapter 3).

An expert witness of course has immunity so far as court appearances are concerned. He is also immune from suit when undertaking connected activities (see Chapter 12). However, he would be well advised to obtain a specific policy of insurance (such as all members of the Academy of Experts must possess) ie, professional indemnity for himself and/or an employee against, eg, dishonesty, a suit for libel and slander, infringement of copyright, negligent loss of documents.

In summary, a policy of professional indemnity insurance is

required by the expert to cover each of the following situations:

(1)   When acting in the normal course of his primary professional business, for any claims which might be taken against him, eg, for negligence.

(2)   When acting as an advisor, ie, as a "shadow expert", to a party on the merits of a claim by or against that party, for any claims that might be made against the expert, eg, for negligent advice.

(3)   When instructed to give or prepare evidence for the purpose of court proceedings as an expert witness. This policy would cover, eg, an expert who does not do the work himself but gives a valuation of the work done. If the expert is legally liable, he would be covered by such a policy.

CHAPTER 14

The Psychiatrist at the Mental Health Review Tribunal - A Specialized Area

*"You deal in the raw material of opinion, and if my convictions
have any validity, opinion ultimately governs the world."*
Woodrow Wilson

The Tribunal

Mental Health Review Tribunals are independent judicial bodies
set up by virtue of the Mental Health Act 1983 as amended by
the Mental Health (Patients in the Community) Act 1995. In
each regional health authority a tribunal is seized of the duty to
review the justification for the continued compulsory detention
of a mentally disordered patient in hospital or the continuation
of guardianship or aftercare under supervision. All compulsory
patients have the right to apply to a Mental Health Review
Tribunal for a review.

So far as an application for discharge is concerned, s.72(l) of
the Mental Health Act 1983 headed "Discharge of Patients",
deals with the powers of the tribunal. The tribunal may in any
case direct that the patient be discharged and:

1. (a) the tribunal shall direct the discharge of a patient liable
        to be detained, under s.2, for assessment if they are

satisfied that he is not suffering from mental disorder, or from a mental disorder of a nature or degree that warrants his detention in a hospital for assessment (or for assessment followed by medical treatment for at least a limited period); or

(b)   that his detention is not justified in the interest of his own health or safety or with a view to the protection of other people.

2. If the patient was admitted to hospital under s.3 of the Act, on the grounds that he was suffering from mental illness requiring treatment, and that it was necessary for the health or safety of the patient, or for the protection of others, that he should receive such treatment then the tribunal shall direct his discharge if satisfied:

(a)   that he is not suffering from mental illness, severe mental impairment, psychopathic disorder or mental impairment and his mental disorder is of a nature or degree which makes it appropriate for him to receive medical treatment in hospital; or

(b)   that it is necessary for the health or safety of the patient or for the protection of other persons that he should receive such treatment.

Where a hospital order is made in respect of an offender by the Crown Court, and it appears to the court, having regard to the nature of the offence, the antecedents of the offender, and the risk of his committing further offences if set at large, that it is necessary for the protection of the public from serious harm to do so, the court may further order that the offender shall be subject to special restrictions, known as "a restriction order" (see s.41 Mental Health Act 1983). Hospital authorities cannot decide whether a patient may move or leave. These are subject to powers exercisable by the Home Secretary and a specially constituted Mental Health Review Tribunal.

Constitution of the Tribunal

Each tribunal consists of a legal chairman, a medical member (who is often a recently retired psychiatrist) and a lay member (who will have experience in administration, knowledge of social services, or possess other qualifications or suitable experience).

The tribunal is not acting as an appellate body against the original decision to admit the patient. It is reviewing the evidence at the time of the hearing to determine whether the patient should be discharged. The patient is the applicant and the onus is on him to prove that the grounds for detaining him do not exist. The tribunal's duty is to balance the crucial issue of the patient's rights and welfare on the one hand with the protection of the public on the other.

Expert Representing the Hospital Authority

The psychiatrist employed by the hospital authority is the Responsible Medical Officer (RMO) in charge of the patient. The RMO is in a unique position as an expert witness in several regards. He is not requested by the patient, the hospital or the tribunal to provide a written report as an independent psychiatrist. He is representing the hospital authority. At any time prior to the hearing before the tribunal he could have discharged the patient; at the hearing he is defending his decision not to have done this.

At the same time - in this essentially legal process - the RMO is, in general terms in exactly the same position as all expert witnesses. At the hearing he must be prepared to answer questions from the tribunal, and from the patient or his legal representative concerning:

    (i)   his current diagnosis;

    (ii)   whether treatment has recently been changed;

    (iii) the justification of his prognosis.

Probity is of overriding importance in all his evidence, whether of fact or opinion. He must possess, and retain throughout, a standard of personal integrity and have the courage to stand by his professional opinion at all costs.

Training to become a psychiatrist does not include instruction on how to achieve a balance, on becoming a responsible medical officer, between:

    (i)   acting as an advocate for the hospital authority - only occasionally will a lawyer be briefed to undertake this task; and

    (ii)   defending his own professional opinion not to release the patient; and

    (iii) assisting the Mental Health Review Tribunal by offering his true and unbiased opinion as an expert.[1]

---

1. Jean Graham Hall and Gordon D. Smith. *New Law Journal*, vol.147, no. 6818, p.1740.

Perception of Responsible Medical Officer's Report

The model form of an expert's report in Appendix II can be used as a basis. It must be used selectively, picking out what is relevant to the particular issues, remembering the context of the tribunal. A well drafted report serves as a good pre-emptive strike in defence of one's opinion.

The statutory requirements set out in the Mental Health Act 1983 must be complied with. The report must include all relevant history including an up-to-date medical report and a social circumstances report from the social worker.

Practical Advice

1. Remember the old military dictum that time spent on reconnaissance is never wasted. Try to see the applicant personally as many times as possible before the hearing. Get to know him personally.
2. Make your own notes at the time of each one of these meetings.
3. Familiarize yourself with the patient's medical records. Nursing records are particularly helpful, providing as they do a day-by-day account of life on the ward.
4. Revise your report as often as necessary, even up to the day of the hearing. If you do this, remember to explain the alterations in detail to the tribunal in your opening remarks.
5. Regard the other members of the staff who are involved as a team. You are in effect the team leader, so make sure you are fully conversant with the contents of the social worker's report, and any other ancillary reports. Also make sure that everybody involved knows what they are doing.

6. Finally, take the case yourself, and do not send your Registrar - even if this means getting someone else to cope with that all-important clinic.

The Independent Psychiatrist

The patient is entitled to call an independent psychiatrist as a witness on his behalf. In that event the independent psychiatrist will see the patient at the hospital in order to write his report and give his evidence, including his opinion, to the tribunal.

Increasingly, use is made by patients and their legal representatives of independent psychiatrists. The general rules pertaining to expert witnesses apply to their reports and conduct before the tribunal.

In *W v. Edgell* (1990) 1 All ER 835 the question arose whether the independent expert is entitled to disclose his report to the hospital authorities and the Home Office, or whether the duty of confidentiality predominates if the patient does not want such report disclosed. It was held that the expert was entitled to disclose his report if, in his professional opinion, this was necessary in the public interest to protect others from possible violence.

The solicitor acting for the patient might wish to obtain a second report, hopefully more to the liking of the patient. If the patient has legal aid, the Legal Services Commission would have to be informed - it is not the policy of the Legal Services Commission to fund a search for a report from an expert who favours the point of view of the applicant.

The independent psychiatrist has a difficult role. Although he is entitled to have a sight of all medical records, he probably will have seen the patient only on one occasion (unlike the RMO who will have had the opportunity to see the patient on a number of occasions and also discuss the matter with other members of the hospital staff.[2])

The Hearing

This is held in private, with everyone seated. The chairman of the tribunal explains in simple terms the duty of the tribunal and how it intends to proceed.

As the application is made by or on behalf of the patient, who must make out a case for discharge, it might be expected that the applicant starts first. However, the solicitor (or barrister) for the applicant (who will be legally aided) may want the Responsible Medical Officer to begin. We advise that the RMO enters into discussions with the legal representative of the patient before the hearing. The RMO can then make it clear that whilst he is prepared to start first, he intends to make an opening statement; and requests the tribunal for permission to do so.

The tribunal will have read all submitted reports previous to the hearing.

The chairman will probably ask the RMO if he has anything to add to his report, then put questions to him. After that, the legal representative of the patient will ask questions.

The medical member of the tribunal will ask specifically medical questions, and the lay member ask questions dealing with social matters.

---

2. *Ibid.*

After all the evidence (not on oath) has been given for the hospital authority, the same process will take place on behalf of the patient.

The patient, or his legal representative, is entitled to the last word.

The tribunal then requests everyone to withdraw so it might consider the evidence. The decision is almost always given in writing later the same day in the absence of the patient and any others who attended. The decision may be given orally, although this is unusual.

Cross Examination of the Responsible Medical Officer

The most relevant questions the RMO should expect and be prepared to answer:

(i)   Is the patient now suffering from a mental disorder within the meaning of the Act?

(ii)   Assuming the answer to the previous question is yes. Which?

(iii)   Is the mental disorder of a nature or degree which makes it appropriate for him to be detained in hospital for medical treatment? (The question may be split into two, as nature and degree are separate considerations.)

(iv)   In the case of psychopathic disorder or mental impairment. Is such treatment likely to alleviate or prevent a deterioration in his condition?

(v)   Is it necessary for the health or safety of the patient or for the protection of others (and if so, which) that he continues to be detained under the section?

(vi)   Why not discharge the patient?

(vii) When did you last examine the patient?

(viii) What progress has the patient made since the date of your last report?

(ix)   What steps are you now taking (ie, trying new drugs)?

(x)   Why has the patient not improved?

(xi)   Why not discharge the patient completely when you recently allowed him two days home leave?

(xii) What are the relevant features of your care plan for this patient?

(xiii) What arrangements have you made for after-care services to be available?

Cross Examination by the RMO of the Independent Psychiatrist: Suggested Questions

(i)   Have you read all the papers?

(ii)   How many times have you seen the patient?

(iii) Did you know that the patient was extremely violent the day after you saw him?

It is possible to think up more aggressive and searching questions The criteria is: will they assist the tribunal in coming to its decision? We advise calmness in the face of aggressive questioning. The legal representative of the patient also has a difficult, and often hopeless, role to play.

The applicant may himself wish to question the independent witness, and is fully entitled to do so.

Aftermath of the Tribunal's Decisions

At the time of the tribunal, if the patient decides to exercise his right to have the last word, albeit against legal advice, all his pent up emotions may be vented on the RMO. He probably regards the RMO as an ogre who has the power to grant freedom but perversely decides to withhold it.

If the tribunal then finds against the patient in his application for discharge, treatment of the patient may run into difficulty. The Responsible Medical Officer will continue to have on-going care for the patient who may be very angry, uncooperative and disgruntled.

The RMO, with his responsibility to conduct the case for the hospital at the tribunal, coupled with his duty as an expert witness and adviser, would be less than human if he too did not feel misunderstood, and sometimes threatened, by those he is sincerely trying to help.

CHAPTER 15

The Integrity of the Expert Witness

"If everyone were clothed with integrity, if every heart were just, and frank and friendly, the other virtues would be well-nigh useless."

Moliére: Le Misanthrope (1666)

The need for the expert witness to possess and retain a standard of absolute personal integrity is a subject to which we make no apology for dwelling upon at some length. The expert witness must have the courage to stand by his professional opinion at all costs. He must resist the temptation to have his report tailored, and thereby tarnished, to suit the needs of the client. His overriding duty is to the court; if this was not already abundantly clear it is stressed in the *Access to Justice* Report and in the consequent Civil Procedures Rules 1998.

Criticism by the Courts

Formerly courts have expressed their views in no uncertain terms although sometimes their words fell upon deaf ears. In *Whitehouse v. Jordan* both the Court of Appeal and the House of Lords dealt with the matter in terms of some scathing detail. That was a case in which the claimant, who was born with severe brain damage, claimed this had been caused by the professional negligence of the senior registrar of the hospital at the time of birth. The Court of Appeal and then the House of Lords held that the evidence was not of sufficient strength to lead to a finding of professional negligence.

In the Court of Appeal [1980] 1 All ER 65 referring to the report of two experts, Lord Denning said:

"In the first place, their joint report suffers to my mind from the way it was prepared. It was the result of long conferences between two professors and counsel in London, and was actually 'settled' by counsel. In short, it wears the colours of special pleading rather than an impartial report. Whenever counsel 'settle' documents we know how it goes. 'We had better put this in.' 'We had better leave this out,' and so forth. A striking instance is the way in which Professor Tizard's was 'doctored'. The lawyers blocked out a couple of lines in which he agreed with Professor Strang that there was no negligence."

In the House of Lords [1981] 1 WLR 246, having dealt with the issue in the case, Lord Wilberforce said:

"One final word. I have to say I feel some concern as to the manner in which part of the expert evidence called for the plaintiff came to be organized. The matter was discussed in the Court of Appeal and commented on by Lord Denning. While some degree of consultation between experts and legal advisers is entirely proper, it is necessary that expert evidence presented to the court should be, and should be seen to be, the independent product of the expert, uninfluenced as to the form or content by the exigencies of litigation. To the extent that it is not, the evidence is likely to be not only incorrect but self-defeating."

Criticism of expert witnesses by the courts goes back a long way. In *Lord Abinger v. Ashton* [1874] 22 WR 582, Sir George Jessel said:

"In matters of opinion I very much distrust expert evidence, for several reasons. In the first place, although the evidence is given upon oath, in point of fact the person knows that he cannot be indicted for perjury, because it is only evidence as to a matter of opinion. So that you have not the authority of legal sanction. A dishonest man, knowing he could not be punished, might be inclined to indulge in extravagant assertions on an occasion that required it. But that is not all. Expert evidence of this kind is evidence of persons who sometimes live by their business, but in all cases are remunerated for their evidence. An expert is not like an ordinary witness, who hoped to get his expenses, but he is employed and paid in the sense of gain, being employed by the person who calls him. Now it is natural that his mind, however honest he may be, should be biased in favour of the person employing him, and accordingly we do find such bias ... Undoubtedly there is a natural bias to do something serviceable for those who employ you and adequately remunerate you. It is very natural, and it is so effectual that we constantly see persons, instead of considering themselves witnesses, rather consider themselves as the paid agents of the person who employs them."

In *Kennard v. Ashman* [1894] 10 TLR 213 Willis J found himself in a classical predicament concerning the condition of a house.

The Rev. R.B. Kennard the lessor of Bella Vista, Harrow, claimed from the defendant the Rev. J.W. Ashman the lessee, the sum of £55, being one quarter's rent, plus £29.34 being six month's interest alleged to be due. The defendant admitted the lease, but claimed to have it set aside for misrepresentation by the lessor's agent, his son, who had stated that: (1) the house was well built, (2) it was in good and tenantable condition and (3) its sanitary condition was perfect. The headnote to the case states that the evidence of the surveyors was so contradictory that the learned Judge said he despaired of ascertaining the true facts of the case from their evidence. The Judge adjourned the hearing in order that Mr Pilditch, an independent surveyor nominated by the Judge, should report upon the state of the house. In his judgment Willis J said "In the opinion of Mr Pilditch the house was not well built, the mortar was indifferent, the damp-course was not a good one, and there was a want of effective concreting over the area of excavation occupied by the house, which rendered it cold and damp and not fit for a tenant to inhabit with reasonable regard to health and comfort."

Impact of the Civil Procedure Rules

The Rules should make a great difference to the professional standing of the expert witness. They emphasize his independence whether he is party appointed or is a single joint expert, eg, R.35(6) allows a party to put written questions about his report to:

(a)   an expert instructed by another party; or
(b)   a single joint expert.

Use of the single joint expert is likely to increase. In *Re B (A Minor) (Sexual Abuse Expert's Report)* (2000) *The Times,* March 29, the Court of Appeal emphasized the importance of instructions to an expert in sexual abuse cases to prepare a report for the proceedings being impartial and made jointly.

A single joint expert may feel the need for advice on certain issues. He cannot rely on counsel to help him draft his report. However, he has the right to ask the Court for directions (R.35. 14) and he may do this without giving notice to any party.

The day of the "amenable" expert who can "be relied upon" is over. The future of well qualified professional people, expert and still working in their primary profession is bright, so long as experts realise that they can expect to encounter equally well-qualified colleagues on numerous occasions, and to meet the same solicitors again and again. A reputation for integrity can easily be burnished or tarnished by tap-room gossip founded on fact. We would remind our readers that Judges are gregarious creatures and the shake of a head or the tightening of a lip at the mention of the name of an expert who had recently given evidence in a case conveys to his colleagues the judgment based on a lifetime of listening and evaluating witnesses. Naturally we would prefer to believe that the readers of this book guarded honour for its own sake in their professional relationships coupled with pride in well-presented expert evidence. On such foundations do personal reputations rest.

Postscript

"In this world second thoughts, it seems, are best."
Hippolytus: 428 BC

We have tried in this book to communicate all we consider relevant to the subject within the confines of our terms of reference. However if, gentle reader, you are still with us we close with extracts from two other books which we feel encapsulate on the one hand the qualities of the ideal expert witness, and on the other virtually everything we have tried to demonstrate must be avoided.

The first is a description by the late Sir Travers Humphreys, when a distinguished Judge, of Sir Bernard Spilsbury, a pathologist who gave evidence at most of the celebrated murder trials in the first half of the century. Sir Travers, when treasury counsel, worked with Spilsbury on a number of those cases and subsequently sat as a Judge hearing his evidence in other trials. He wrote:

"Spilsbury in the witness-box was to my mind the ideal scientific witness. He was unemotional, simple in speech because he was clear in mind, absolutely fair, quite indifferent to the result of a case, paying little or no attention to those parts of the evidence which did not affect the medical or scientific aspects of the matter. He spared no pains in seeking out anything, fact, theory, or latest discovery, which could properly affect his judgment. He learned from Willcox early in his career the art of helping a muddled or halting cross-examiner to put his questions in such a way as to enable the witness to agree with his proposition. A frequent answer of his in the witness-box would be: 'Put in that way, I am afraid I cannot agree; but if you ask whether the evidence is consistent with such and such a theory, you are quite right.' At one time medical and legal critics thought that Spilsbury was becoming too didactic, but I think it must have come to his notice, for he quickly reverted to his old formula, 'I have no doubt' or 'That is the most modern view.' His own knowledge of his subject was, of course, immense. His medical colleagues will no doubt testify to that, and to his pre-eminence as a lecturer." (*Bernard Spilsbury: His Life and Cases* by Douglas G. Browne and E.V. Tullett, published by George G. Hannay & Co. Ltd)

By way of total contrast, the second extract is from *Daddy's Girl* by Clifford Irving (published by Hodder and Stoughton, 1988), a book on the Campbell murder case that aroused considerable controversy in the USA in the mid-1980s. In a short cross-examination the unfortunate Dr Owens provides a well-nigh perfect illustration of what not to do:

"Dr Owens was not a prepossessing figure. He had a thick body and short legs, and he couldn't keep his white shorts tucked into his trousers. But facing Rusty, he squared his shoulders and thrust out his jaw.

And well he might. Rusty was on a roll, ready for a scrap.

He began by asking what books or articles or papers the psychologist had written on the subject of child abuse.

None.

None?

None.

Well, what had he read?

Dr Owens couldn't remember.

Rusty gave him ample time, but Owens only looked more and more befuddled. He was terribly sorry, but he just couldn't remember, he had a mental block. Not a single book? Not a single article?

No ... sorry.

From the defence table, Allen stared at the doctor uncomprehending. Allen's stomach was churning.

He hadn't come prepared, Dr Owens explained, to cite the authorities. Rusty took the risk and asked: What had he come prepared for?

'I came prepared to give the benefit of my academic experience in a general way.'

In the Texas Department of Corrections he had been in classification, in diagnostics and evaluation. 'No,' he admitted, 'there were no abused children *per se* at TDC.'

The more flustered Dr Owens became, the more he reverted to multisyllabic words and academic jargon. In earning his master's degree, had he taken any course in child abuse? Well, his master's degree had been in the subject of rehabilitation.

'Of whom?'

'It was in the subject of location evaluation ... it was a multidisciplinary degree.'

'Does that mean you were studying the prison system?'

'It does not mean that per se.'

'What does it mean' - Rusty tried not to smile - 'per se?'

'Psychometric testing of individuals ... modalities ... identifying specific syndromes.'

'Is that child abuse? Did you study child abuse for your master's?'

'If you're asking was there a specific course entitled Child Abuse, no.'

Ditto for his undergraduate work and Ph.D. As for his practice as a psychologist, no, it had never been devoted to child abusers or abused children.

In one long sentence, area by area, Rusty summoned up Owen's preparation, education, and current expertise in the field of child abuse - or rather, his striking lack of it - and ending up by asking:

'Is that a fair statement?'

'I would perhaps objects to one comment', said Dr Owens, 'but except for that, yes, that's a fair statement.'

'What's the comment you object to?'

'I don't recall it specifically.' Dr Owens said.

'Thank you, Doctor,' said Rusty. 'I have no further questions.'"

(Reproduced with the kind permission of the Publishers).

APPENDIX I

Checklist for the Nervous Novice

There is nothing worse than arriving for the hearing late, flustered and uncertain that you have brought everything you may need. Before moving off, we suggest that you calmly and deliberately check you have the following:

1. The Report/Proof - and all the copies required.
2. The file of the case.
3. The exhibits - with all copies references and in the correct order.
4. Textbook/reference books.
5. Pen/spare pen and notebook/spare paper.
6. Map of the tribunal location.
7. If travelling by car ask yourself:

    (a)   Is there an *available* car park at the tribunal?
    (b)   If not, proximity of the nearest public car park.
    (c)   Are there any road-works, or have there been accidents that day? (Check early morning TV and radio reports.)

8. If travelling by public transport check:

    (a)   Distance from railway/bus station.
    (b)   Times of trains/buses.

(c) Public transport failures and cancellations (TV and radio reports).

9. Time of hearing - plan to arrive between 30-60 minutes earlier.
10. Cash - including small change for parking meters and telephone calls.
11. On arrival at the tribunal:

    (a) Go to the loo first!
    (b) Enlist the help of the court usher to find out which court you are in and to meet up with your instructing solicitor.

12. Take other work with you - you may well have to wait some time.
13. Remind your solicitor if the case runs on you are not available tomorrow afternoon.
14. Having carefully read this book - follow our advice!

Model Form of Expert's Report

(Reproduced by the kind permission of the Academy of Experts)

[SHORT TITLE OF ACTION]
[DRAFT]
REPORT OF
[EXPERT'S NAME]
DATED
[   ]

Specialist field:	[State title of specialism]
Assisted by:	[State names of assistants]
On behalf of:	[State party's name]
On instruction of:	[State name of those instructing]
Subject matter:	[State briefly the nature of the matter and the date when it arose]
Interview date(s):	[Give the dates or period of all interviews]

[Name, Address and Occupation of the writer's practice (if any) and telephone, fax, DX and reference]

(1.00 Introduction)   Report of   :
                          Specialist field   :
                          On behalf of   :

CONTENTS
[Change or omit as appropriate]

(1.00 Introduction)   Report of   :
                               Specialist field   :
                               On behalf of   :

REPORT

1.00 INTRODUCTION

1.01 Formal Details

[Note 1 - state (as applicable) your full name. Give your status (eg, partner of), the name of your firm, the nature of its business and its address.]

[Note 2 - state your own specialist field; there is provision later on for you to deal with qualifications, experience etc.]

[Note 3 - state on behalf of whom you were instructed and the name, address and business of those instructing you.]

1.02 Synopsis

[Note 1 - Set out concisely the general nature of the dispute, eg, "In this case, Ambridge Cricket Club alleges faulty design and erection of a new cricket pavilion." The main areas of complaint relate to the roof and verandah. I am advising the engineers. There are also complaints against the architects.]

1.03 Instructions

[Note 1 - State briefly what you have been asked to do, eg, "to identify the issues within my specialist field that arise in this case, to make a technical investigation and to express my opinion with full reason in each issue".]

1.04 Disclosure of Interests

[Note 1 - State any actual or potential conflict of interests that you may have, for example a connection with any of the parties or witnesses or advisers which might be thought to influence the opinions expressed in the report.]

[Note 2 - State (if it is so) that you have no such connexion with any of the parties, witnesses or advisers involved in the case.]

1.05 Appendix 1 - contains details of my experience, qualifications, appointments and specialist field(s) [together with those of ( ) who has/have assisted me in (state the areas of assistance).]

[Note 1 - every person who has been involved in the investigation or inquiry and who has formed opinions on which the writer of the report is relying must be identified here and their details provide at Appendix 1.]

1.06 Appendix 2 - contains a list of some of the documents I have considered together with copies of only those documents which I regard as essential for the understanding of my report.

[Note 1 - every effort should be made to limit the number of documents which are added to the report.]

[Note 2 - where documents are bulky they should be listed shortly by reference to bundles and not individually.]

1.07 Appendix 3 - contains a list of the texts and published material to which I have referred in this report. I have included some copies or extracts for ease of reference.

1.08 Appendix 4 - contains a list and copies of the [photographs, drawings, laboratory reports, schedules etc.] which [name of assistant and/or] I have prepared for the purposes of this report.

1.09 Appendix 4 - contains [a full chronology].

1.10 Appendix 6 - contains [etc. as/if applicable].

(2.00 Background/Issues)	Report of	:
	Specialist field	:
	On behalf of	:

2.00   THE BACKGROUND TO THE DISPUTE AND THE ISSUES

2.01   The Relevant Parties
[Note 1 - set out briefly in short itemized paragraphs the names of those to whom you will refer in this report, together with a short, uncontroversial statement of their role in the relevant events.]

[Note 2 - please avoid acronyms. For example, the firm name Smith Jones Brown & Co. Limited may better be shortened to "Smith" than "SJBCL".]

2.02   The Assumed Facts
[Note 1 - set out in short itemized paragraphs a background narrative of the facts you have been asked to assume.]

[Note 2 - bear in mind that a full chronology, if

appropriate, will be provided at Appendix 5.]

2.03 The Issues to be addressed

[Note 1 - identify, in short itemized paragraphs, each of the allegations and issues that you will, in turn, address. Say where in the case papers it arises and which party has raised it.]

[Note 2 - where practicable, keep the list of issues raised by one party separate from those raised by any other party.]

[Note 3 - this part of the report is factual only; no opinion should be expressed here.]

(3.00 Investigation)   Report of   :
                                      Specialist Field   :
                                      On behalf of   :

3.00 THE TECHNICAL INVESTIGATION [INQUIRY]

[Note 1 - give in short itemized paragraphs the date(s), and time(s) of day you attended to investigate the factual position. State where you went, what you saw and did and who assisted you, who else was present and what you found.]

[Note 2 - it is desirable to avoid reporting second or third hand hearsay; this is not, however, an inflexible rule. There may be occasions when reliable hearsay should be reported. State in each case the name of the person who relayed the hearsay.]

[Note 3 - experiments, detailed surveys, measurements, audits etc. should be briefly described. The full report should appear as an Appendix.]

[Note 4 - this section of the report is factual only; no opinion should be expressed.]

(*4.00 Factual Basis*)   Report of   :
                                   Specialist Field :
                                   On behalf of   :

4.00 THE FACTS ON WHICH THE EXPERT'S OPINION IS BASED

[Note 1 - identify separately and distinguish between:
a) facts which the writer has been asked to assume;
b) facts which the writer observed for himself, eg, the results of experiments, investigations etc. carried out by the writer himself;
c) facts which others, acting on behalf of the writer, observed (and identify the persons concerned);
d) the opinions of others upon which the writer relied in forming his own opinion.]

[Note 2 - refer as convenient to any rules, regulations or other documentary guidance which you consider to be relevant. Where essential, these should be copies at Appendix 3.]

(*5.00 Conclusions*)   Report of   :
                                   Specialist Field :
                                   On behalf of   :

5.00 CONCLUSIONS

5.01 [Set out the first issue and your opinion on that issue with reasons in full.]

[Note 1 - if applicable provide a sub-heading for each of the issues.]

[Note 2 - provide cross references to the text or any published material which supports the conclusions.]

[Note 3 - only refer to matters of fact so far as may be necessary to the understanding of the opinion.]

5.02 [Continue to set out each issue in turn with opinion and full reasons following the notes given above.]

Signature . . . . Name in full . . . . Date . . . .

APPENDIX 1

Report of   :
Specialist field   :
On behalf of   :

CONTENTS

1.
2.
3.
4.

© The Academy of Experts, South Square, Grays Inn, London WC1 RHP.

APPENDIX III

The Academy of Expert's Form of Expert's Declaration

THIS DECLARATION SHOULD BE INSERTED BETWEEN THE END OF THE REPORT AND THE EXPERT'S SIGNATURE.

I . . . . DECLARE THAT:
[INSERT FULL NAME]

1. I understand that my primary duty in written reports and giving evidence is to the Court, rather than the party who engaged me.
2. I have endeavoured in my reports and in my opinions to be accurate and to have covered all relevant issues concerning the matters stated which I have been asked to address.
3. I have endeavoured to include in my report those matters, which I have knowledge of or of which I have been made aware, that might adversely affect the validity of my opinion.
4. I have indicated the sources of all information I have used.
5. I have not without forming an independent view included or excluded anything which has been suggested to me by others (in particular my instructing lawyers).
6. I will notify those instructing me immediately and confirm in writing if for any reason my existing report requires any correction or qualification.
7. I understand that:

a) my report, subject to any corrections before swearing as to its correctness, will form the evidence to be given under oath or affirmation;
b) I may be cross-examined on my report by a cross-examiner assisted by an expert;
c) I am likely to be the subject of public criticism by the judge if the Court concludes that I have not taken reasonable care in trying to meet the standards set out above.

8. I confirm that I have not entered into any arrangement where the amount or payment of my fees is in any way dependent on the outcome of the case.

Arbitration and Independent Expert Determination
Contrasted

Arbitrator

1. Subject to the provisions of the Arbitration Act 1996.
2. Objective is to determine dispute that has arisen.
3. Must hold hearing unless parties agree otherwise.
4. Judicial role: hears parties' submissions/evidence, and must observe rules of natural justice.
5. May take evidence on oath or affirmation.
6. Either party may apply for disclosure or to subpoena witnesses.
7. Must make award strictly on evidence presented: must not use special knowledge.
8. Can be compelled to give reasons.
9. Award may be enforced by action on the award or as a judgment.
10. Not liable for anything done or omitted in discharge of his functions (except in bad faith).

Independent Expert

1. Not specifically subject to statute.
2. Objective is to decide between parties' opposing interests so that dispute may be avoided.
3. Need not hold hearing (unless so required by terms of appointment).
4. No duty to take account of parties' representations, rules of evidence do not apply.
5. Evidence not given on oath.
6. Neither party can apply for disclosure or subpoena.
7. Need not take account of parties' representations in reaching decision; can employ own expertise, knowledge or information.
8. Cannot be compelled to give reasons unless specific requirements in terms of appointment.
9. Determination forms part of a contract between parties: can only be enforced by further action.
10. Liable for negligence as in other forms of his professional work.

Index

UK Expert List

www.ukexpertlist.com

the expert witness directory

Getting yourself known for medico-legal or pharmaceutical company work can be difficult. Equally, lawyers and pharmaceutical companies need assistance finding the right doctor. UK Expert List's team of practising lawyers and medics have teamed up to produce a new simple-to-use website designed to work as you work.

Experts – Do You Want to be Found? – *Introductory offer*

Experts – make sure you can be found with a few minutes spent registering.

- *FREE INTRODUCTORY OFFER: until 31 October 2006 full listing will be free of charge.*
- After this, basic listing will remain free
- be promoted heavily to the legal profession and other interested groups through publications such as *Personal Injury Brief Update,* the highest circulation in the PI industry

Full details are on our site at www.ukexpertlist.com – but if you would like to discuss any of the details you find there, we can be contacted on 0870 143 2569.

Looking for an Expert?

Rapidly find a selection of experts and then allowing you to filter them.

- No need to register
- No fees
- Filter by location and keywords.

Printed in the United Kingdom
by Lightning Source UK Ltd.
114139UKS00001B/103-132